The Christmas Story

ILLUSTRATED BY STEPHANIE RYDER

B R I M A X

Long ago, in a town called Nazareth, there lived a young woman named Mary. One day a great light appeared and the angel Gabriel stood before her. "Do not be afraid," said the angel. "I bring you joyful news. God has chosen you to be the mother of his son. You will have a baby and you must call him Jesus."

In the same town there lived a
carpenter named Joseph.
Joseph loved Mary very much.
He was going to marry her.
The angel came to visit Joseph
and told him that Mary was
going to have God's son. Later
Joseph came to see Mary and
told her what the angel had
said.

One day a message came from the governor of the land. All of the people had to go back to the place where they had been born so they could be counted. Joseph was worried. He and Mary would have to go to Bethlehem. This was a long way away and Mary was almost ready to have her baby.

They set off early the next morning. Joseph led the way. Mary rode on a donkey. The road was long and hard. They didn't reach Bethlehem until the evening. The town was full of people. Joseph tried everywhere to find a place to stay, but all the rooms were taken. Mary was so tired she could hardly stay awake.

At last an innkeeper said, "All my rooms are full, but you can use my stable. It is clean and warm in there."
Joseph thanked him and they went inside. All around them cows and donkeys lay peacefully asleep. The hay was soft and smelled sweet. Mary and Joseph lay down and rested.

In the night, Mary gave birth
to her baby. It was a boy as
the angel had said. They
named him Jesus.
Mary wrapped him in
a blanket and laid him in
a manger, where it was soft
and warm.
Mary and Joseph watched over
Jesus lovingly. They knew he
was a very special baby.

Out on the hillside above the town, some shepherds were looking after their sheep. Suddenly the sky was filled with light and an angel appeared. The shepherds fell to the ground in fear.

But the angel said, "Do not be afraid. I bring you good news. Today a child is born. He is the son of God. You will find him in Bethlehem, lying in a manger."

The shepherds gazed in wonder as the sky was filled with angels singing.

"We must go and find this child," said one. "We can take one of our newborn lambs as a gift."

They went to Bethlehem and found Jesus in the stable with Mary and Joseph. They fell to their knees and offered their gift.

Far away in an eastern land lived some wise men. One night they saw a bright new star in the sky. They wanted to know what it meant. They looked in their books for the answer. "It means that a new king has been born," they said. "We must go and look for him so that we can worship him. The star will guide us."

The wise men set off on their journey. The star shone brightly in front of them by day and by night. They came to the palace of King Herod who said to them, "You must find the new king then tell me where he is." King Herod was not very pleased.

The wise men followed
the star for many miles. It
stopped right over the stable
where Jesus lay. "We are
looking for the newborn king,"
they said. "A bright star has
guided us from far away."
Joseph led them into the
stable. They knelt before Jesus
and offered him some very
special gifts of gold,
frankincense and myrrh.

The next day, the wise men set out for King Herod's palace. They stopped to rest and while they were asleep an angel came to them in a dream. "Do not go back to Herod," the angel warned. "He does not want Jesus to be King." The wise men decided to go home a different way.

Mary and Joseph were very happy and proud. They knew their baby was really the son of God. They knew he was very special and that he would have important work to do when he grew up. They also knew that Jesus would be loved throughout the world and that people would remember his birth as a time of happiness and peace.

Say these words again.

carpenter	star
message	palace
donkey	special
stable	dream
blanket	happiness
sheep	bright
gift	worship

OE ON THE SHORE
area Lewis and Clark,
met the first American
dvancing into the great
Louisiana Territory,
rs before acquired by
tes.

LAGES

ORTH DAKOTA

S

VILLAGES

SOUTH DAKOTA

PIERRE

Riviere au Jacques

THE SIX TURNINGS
IN THE AMERICAN WEST
1806 - 1834

MINNESOTA

IOWA

OMAHAS

KA

COUNCIL BLUFFS

ILLINOIS

Platte R.

Big Blue R.

ilding
mie),
stem.
anent
trade,
tions.

KANSAS

Missouri R.

IV — MONOPOLY ON THE MISSOURI
In 1822 big business and national political
power reached the West when Astor's Western
Department of the American Fur Company
entered and soon monopolized the fur trade
of the Missouri River and of St. Louis.

Mississippi R.

Kansas R.

WESTPORT
INDEPENDENCE

ST. LOUIS

KANSAS

TRAIL

III — A STRANGE NEW VOICE
In 1817 the first steamboat reached St.
Louis. Two years later came the first
attempt to navigate the Missouri River.

MISSOURI

Other Books by
JOHN UPTON TERRELL

LA SALLE: a biography of America's greatest explorer

ZEBULON PIKE: the life and times of an adventurer

ESTEVANICO THE BLACK: discoverer of Arizona and New Mexico

TRADERS OF THE WESTERN MORNING: aboriginal commerce in
   pre-Columbian North America

WAR FOR THE COLORADO RIVER: California-Arizona, and the
   Upper Basin. 2 volumes

BLACK ROBE: a biography of Pierre-Jean de Smet, first Rocky
   Mountain missionary

FURS BY ASTOR: a history of John Jacob Astor and the American fur trade

FAINT THE TRUMPET SOUNDS: the life and trials of Major Reno

JOURNEY INTO DARKNESS: the story of Cabeza de Vaca

PUEBLO OF THE HEARTS: the story of Pueblo de Corazones

Western Lands and Waters Series
VIII

THE SIX TURNINGS

*major changes in the
American West*

1806-1834

by
John Upton Terrell

THE ARTHUR H. CLARK COMPANY
Glendale, California   1968

Contents

AUTHOR'S NOTE 9

1806 – TURNING NUMBER ONE . . 13
A CANOE ON THE SHORE: The first Mountain Men go
out, and the American fur trade begins in the Far
West

1810 – TURNING NUMBER TWO . . 83
THE WIDE HORIZON: Private capital for the first time
attempts to expand the American economic empire to
the Columbia Basin and North Pacific Coast

1817 – TURNING NUMBER THREE . . 107
A STRANGE NEW VOICE OF HOPE AND DOOM: The
steamboat reaches the Missouri River and revolutionizes western commerce

1822 – TURNING NUMBER FOUR . . 137
MONOPOLY ON THE MISSOURI: The insuperable alliance
of big business and national political power reaches
the West

1824 – TURNING NUMBER FIVE . . 167
RENDEZVOUS IN THE MOUNTAINS: Introduction of new
systems of supply and transport drastically change the
far western fur trade

1834 – TURNING NUMBER SIX . . 211
CROSSROADS: Private forts, built at strategic locations in
the mountains, supersede the rendezvous, serve the
western fur trade the year round, and become supply,
repair and trading centers of a new economic era —
The era of mass migration

INDEX 245

Author's Note

This is a book almost entirely about the early American West. It touches only briefly on the trans-Mississippi region under France and Spain, and it refers only incidentally to the Spanish Provinces of the Southwest and the Pacific Coast.

In writing it, I have adhered to a pattern and sought a specific goal. The period covered embraces the first thirty years after the purchase by the United States of Louisiana Territory, but the work must not be regarded as a general history of that period, for it most definitely is not. Rather, it is a recounting of certain events which took place in those years and which were of impressive consequence.

There were, I believe, in those three decades, six important turnings in the road leading America toward the western sun. Each of them not only gave new direction to that road, but opened the way to essential transitions in the thoughts and actions of the travelers upon it. Moreover, each turning brought new conflicts — economic, social and political — that significantly influenced the entire nation as it moved toward its "manifest destiny."

JOHN UPTON TERRELL

1806

TURNING NUMBER ONE

———◆———

A Canoe on the Shore

The first Mountain Men go out,
and the American fur trade
begins in the Far West

I

A Canoe on the Shore

At noon they proceeded on about two miles,
when they observed a canoe near the shore.
They immediately landed, and were equally
surprised and pleased at discovering two men
by the names of Dickson and Hancock,
who had come from the Illinois on a
hunting expedition   .   .   .

Those words may be found in the journals of Lewis
and Clark. They were written on Wednesday, the 11th
of August, 1806, a few miles below the confluence of
the Yellowstone and Missouri rivers, when the first
American expendition to break a trail to the Pacific was
on its way home.[1]

The simplicity of the entry disguises its true meaning.
Perhaps, as he scratched his pen on the soiled paper

---

[1] *The Journals of Lewis and Clark* are in large part uninteresting, tedious
and difficult to follow. Professional analysis and interpretation are needed
to emphasize and define the innumerable points and qualities which make
them documents of incomparable historical value. Also, without this guid-
ance one inevitably becomes hopelessly lost in a geographical labyrinth.
See Elliott Coues, *History of the Expedition under . . . Lewis and Clark*,
4 vols., New York, 1893; Reuben G. Thwaites, ed., *Original Journals of the
Lewis and Clark Expedition*, 8 vols., New York, 1904-05, and reprint, 1959;
John Bartlett Brebner, *Explorers of North America*, London, 1933; Patrick
Gass, *Journal of Voyages and Travels . . .* , Pittsburgh, 1807, and reprints:
Olin D. Wheeler, *The Trail of Lewis and Clark*, 2 vols., New York, 1904.
The Heritage Press, New York, in 1962 reprinted in two illustrated volumes
the Nicholas Biddle edition of *History of the Expedition . . .* which was
published in 1814.

while a mist of mosquitoes tortured him, the writer thought only of completing the duty of recording the day's events. Yet, both tone and text of the diaries nullify the suggestion that Meriwether Lewis and William Clark were not aware of the economic as well as the historical importance of most incidents and events, major and minor, which occurred on their epic journey.

The significance of the meeting with the two trappers stemmed no more from its reality than from its prognostication.

The first American Mountain Men had reached the Yellowstone, on the edge of a wilderness which, except for the few eyes of the Lewis and Clark Expedition that had gazed briefly across a fragment of its perimeter, had never been seen by men of the white race.

The door to the first delineative period of the early history of the American West had been pushed ajar. It would never again be closed.

Through this door soon would pass a ragged parade – individuals, small bands and large companies – comprised of men whose daring was as incomparable as their adventures and accomplishments were unbelievable. They were the precursors of the American fur trade of the Far West. They were a kind, a breed, a loosely-knitted fraternity who gave to the story of American expansion not only a vital and dramatic chapter, but a new way of life, new customs, new ideas, new visions and, undoubtedly without premeditation, molded the foundation of a dynamic new economy.

Little information about Joseph Dickson and Forrest Hancock survived them. Most certainly descendants of Anglo-Saxon pioneers, almost nothing of their personal backgrounds, their appearances or their characters remained to portray them after they went their earthly ways. Clark's account states merely that they "left the Illinois [presumably the river] in the summer of 1804, and had spent the last winter with the Tetons [Sioux], in company with a Mr. Ceautoin, who had come there as a trader   .   .   ."

Revealing is the reference found in other accounts that they also had been among the Cheyennes, and were eager to visit more remote regions. That assertion, while not extraordinary, gives them a quality which explains to some extent why they were pushing up the Missouri, some seventeen hundred miles above its mouth, when Lewis and Clark met them. The urge to look into the next unknown valley, to go where no man of their kind had ever gone before, impelled the Mountain Men as the dream of plunder and conquest drove the Indian onto the warpath. In both, these things were inherent and irresistible.

Dickson and Hancock remained four days with the expedition. About the campfires they talked of their plan to spend the winter on the upper Missouri. The ears of a young man, an accomplished hunter and a conscientious soldier, were attentive. He questioned them, and his apparently sincere interest in their proposal brought an invitation to remain with them.

On August 14, John Colter made his decision, and the expedition journal tells of it this way:

> In the evening we were applied to by one of our men, Colter, who was desirous of joining the two trappers   .   .   . as he had always performed his duty, and his services might be dispensed with, we agreed that he might go.   .   .   We,

therefore, supplied him, as did his comrades also, with powder
and lead, and a variety of articles which might be useful to
him, and he left us the next day.

With that military discharge on the upper Missouri
River in the summer of 1806, John Colter began a career
of adventure and discovery that was to amaze the civilized world and win for him a place among the greatest
of all western explorers.

Colter, Dickson and Hancock vanished into the wilderness, but if the event was the first of its kind the expedition was to experience, it was not the last. As Lewis
and Clark continued on down the great river, other
meetings with ascending American fur hunters occurred.
James Airs and several Canadian *voyageurs* in two
canoes heavily loaded with merchandise were on their
way to trade with the Sioux in opposition to the North
West Company. Near the Little Sioux River the expedition "met a trading boat belonging to Mr. Augustus
Chateau, of St. Louis, with several men, on their way
to trade with the Yanktons. . ."[2]

Next came two perogues whose occupants were unidentified, one bound for the Pawnees and the other for
the domain of the Omahas. On the same day, Friday,
September 12th, they were joined by a "trading party
under Mr. M'Clellan."[3]

---

[2] Auguste Chouteau, one of the founders and first fur traders of St. Louis.
He first saw the site in the winter of 1763 at the age of thirteen, when he
was an aide to Pierre Laclede Liguest, whose firm, Maxent, Laclede and Co.
had been awarded the exclusive right to trade on the Missouri and Mississippi rivers as far north as the mouth of the St. Peters. The expedition
spent the winter at Fort Chartres, and began the building of St. Louis in
February 1764.

[3] Robert McLellan, veteran soldier and frontiersman, who would be one
of the original Astorians. He distinguished himself in the Indian wars in

The Mountain Men were going out. They knew only that the Far West belonged to the United States, and so to all Americans. The door was open to them, and they would have needed nothing more in the way of an inducement to make them pass through it.

But they were drawn also by other irrestistible powers: the forces of their curiosity and enterprise. They wanted answers to a few simple questions: What was out there? What fortunes, what peoples, what mountains, what rivers, what unsolved mysteries were to be found in the unknown reaches of the Missouri's tributaries, and beyond them, in all that vast untrammeled unconquered territory that reached to the Pacific?

The first American Mountain Men brought a crude culture and a rustic economic system across the Mississippi, but in the limitless expanses of the West these things were found wanting. Indeed, for the most part they were unworkable.

The majority of the early American fur traders were products of an eastern woodlands environment. Many of them were natives of the British Isles, and a few came from Belgium and France, but they, too, had gained their wilderness experience in the thick forests of the Great Lakes region, the North West Territories and Lower Canada.

Ohio, and was approaching middle age when he first crossed the Mississippi. As early as 1805 he was trading with the Omahas. In 1807 he formed a partnership with Ramsay Crooks, who would become one of Astor's chief lieutenants. In the fall of that year they led an expedition of eighty men up the Missouri, establishing a post near the Council Bluffs. They became bitter enemies of Manuel Lisa, charging him with turning the Sioux against them and ruining their trade with that Nation.

Neither implements nor the weapons which served so efficiently along the Rappahannock, the Cumberland, the Allegheny, the Ottawa, the Fox, the Illinois were adequate nor adaptable along the Missouri, the Kansas, the Platte, the Big Horn, the Wind, the Green. Chiefly this unsuitability derived from the demands of bigness and space – the bigness of the land and of the living things upon it, the bigness of the rivers and the hills and the mountains, inconceivable space of earth and sky, the distances in which the eyes became lost and which made the mind cringe under the pressure of an incomprehensible magnitude.[4]

However, if in their advance the Mountain Men were forced to transform their ways and supplement their means with new devices, to adopt many habits and customs heretofore totally unknown to them, they did possess the ingenuity and the facilities for modifying and improving the system and the conditions they encountered in the Western wilderness. They brought progress as they themselves learned and changed, and they spoke the final lines of the drama of an age.

There was coral on the *Riviere au Jacques* which had come from the Sandwich Islands. There were mules at the Mandan Villages which had been stolen by Crow raiders from Spanish outposts in the shadows of the

---

[4] See Walter Prescott Webb, *The Great Plains,* Boston, 1931; Frederick J. Turner, *The Frontier in American History,* New York, 1920; Alfred J. Mokler, *Transition of the West,* Chicago, 1927; Katherine Coman, *Economic Beginnings of the Far West,* New York, 1912; Emma H. Blair, *Indian Tribes of the Upper Mississippi Valley and . . . Great Lakes,* Cleveland, 1911; Ray A. Billington, *Westward Expansion,* New York, 1950, and *Far Western Frontier,* New York, 1956; John Bakeless, *The Eyes of Discovery,* New York, 1950; C. W. Alvord and L. Bidgood, *First Explorations of the Trans-Allegheny Region . . . ,* Cleveland, 1912.

Sangre de Cristo Range. There were buffalo robes on
the Columbia which had been taken and dressed on the
Platte. There were walrus teeth from the Bering Sea
on the Little Missouri, Chippewa baskets on the Coeur
d'Alene, moss agates from the Big Horn on the Des
Moines and on the Willamette, bright pigments and
obsidian and colored stones from the painted reaches of
the Yellowstone on the Purgatoire and the Bitter Root
and the Milk and the Red River of the North, feathers
and quills and carved bones from the Snake and the
Okanagan on the Souris and the Minnesota, and the
same adornments and symbols from the Arkansas and
the Kankakee on the Green and the Powder and the
Popo Agie.

The economic changes which the Mountain Men effected came not in the trails as much as in the products.
The age of metal already had begun to supersede the
age of stone in the West when the first of them pushed
out to the Three Forks and across the Shining Mountains. They would complete the mutation, meeting the
last of the aborigines who had never seen either the
white man or the Negro.

Three hundred years had passed since the transition
had begun. It had moved slowly but steadily westward
from the St. Lawrence, where the first iron cooking pot
from Europe had reached a savage land.

The time when Champlain and his young men first
gazed into the western sky beyond Lachine Rapids had
been itself a time of change, of commercial confusion,
political crises and religious controversies. Not long
before that only the nobility and the rich could afford
fine furs, but other classes were beginning to prosper,

to acquire social rights and privileges, and new markets for less valuable pelts were being created. Wolf, bear, buffalo, fox, lynx, raccoon and muskrat were wanted for coats, linings, collars and gloves. For hats, of course, nothing could surpass the American beaver.

Affiliated with this development, in keeping with the time, was the plan to convert the Indians of northern North America to Christianity. This was more than just a wish or a hope. It was a matter which was given realistic action, and which brought serious clashes involving policies, philosophies, tenets and creeds. The kings and the lords, the dukes and the counts, were obliged to give careful thought to it, while at the same time a swiftly expanding economic system known as capitalism was forcing them to give more than casual attention to mercantilism.

Religion and trade, perhaps equally, at least theoretically, in the beginning, drew the eyes of state leaders to the New World. If they hoped and prayed that God Himself would take a hand in resolving the ecclesiastical problems, they were fully aware that only they could devise a practical and successful program for increasing their monetary resources. The capitalistic theory was not especially complicated, and it appeared to be most suitable as a means of developing the potentialities of the unspoiled land across the Atlantic. There an apparently insatiable demand for European goods had been created among the Indians. One could only guess at its future, for neither the number of red people nor the extent of their continent was known. Wild speculations might prove to be conservative.

No problem was really settled or solved, however,

and the fighting began, growing greater and more bloody as the *voyageurs* pushed into the unknown. The black robes squabbled with the gray friars, and tried to outdo each other in saving souls. The traders fought each other to secure the Indians' furs, and the Indians began to fight each other to control distribution of the white man's marvelous merchandise. The St. Lawrence tribes set themselves up as middlemen, and they gouged their brothers of the interior and attempted to prevent them from coming eastward to trade. They became as dishonest and as unscrupulous as their European counterparts. Goods sent inland by Indians were often damaged, the knives chipped, the cloth worn, and the esteemed cooking pot burned black and thin from usage.

The pattern continued a jump or two ahead of the *voyageurs*. Their manufactured miracles were like shadows preceding them as they advanced into the western sun. Ironware and woven cloth and mirrors and bright trinkets were known to the western tribes before the white traders reached them. It should be said as well that the tribes and the great rivers flowing from the west were known to *voyageurs* before they saw them, for Indians talked of their own peoples and their country as they did about the white man's marvels.[5]

---

[5] See H. P. Biggar, *The Voyage of Jacques Cartier*, Ottawa, Canadian Archives, 1924, *Works of Samuel D. Champlain*, Ottawa, 1934, and *The Early Trading Companies of New France*, Toronto, 1901; Edwin O. Wood, *Historic Mackinac*, New York, 1918; Justin Winsor, *Cartier to Frontenac*, Boston, 1894; Reuben G. Thwaites, *Father Marquette*, New York, 1902; B. Sulte, "Notes on Jean Nicolet" in *Wisconsin Historical Collections*, vol. 8, Madison, 1879; F. B. Steck, *The Jolliet-Marquette Expedition*, Quincy, 1928; John G. Shea, *Discovery and Exploration of the Mississippi Valley*, New York, 1852, reprinted 1903; Charles B. Reed, *The First Great Canadian: Pierre Le Moyne, Sieur d'Iberville*, Chicago, 1910; G. D. Saull, ed.,

Many of the names of the Frenchmen who were the first to follow ancient paths into the wilderness that was to become Louisiana Territory were soon forgotten, if, indeed, they were recorded. Some were remembered, but only a very few of these kept accounts, or even took the trouble to report where they had gone or what they had seen. They simply vanished into the West.

Yet, it became known that some, in truth, had been out there and had made certain discoveries. By the end of the seventeenth century *voyageurs* from Canada were trading with the Missouri and Osage Indians. Perhaps as many as a hundred Canadians were living in widely scattered places along the upper Mississippi and upper Missouri. Some had made extraordinary journeys. Some *voyageurs,* whose names are not now known, if they ever were, reportedly had gone far up the Missouri and reached a beautiful country. Word filtered back to Montreal that others had traded with natives who were as fair

Radisson's Voyages, Boston, 1885; Francis Parkman, *LaSalle and the Discovery of the Great West,* Boston, 1879, *The Old Regime in Canada,* Boston, 1874, *Pioneers of France in the New World,* Boston, 1865, *Count Frontenac and New France,* Boston, 1877, *Jesuits in North America,* Boston, 1867, and reprints; F. A. Ogg, *Opening of the Mississippi,* New York, 1904; Grace L. Nute, *Caesars of the Wilderness,* New York, 1943; Marc Lescarbot, *History of New France,* ed. W. L. Grant, 2 vols., Toronto, 1914; Louise P. Kellogg, *Early Narrative of the Northwest,* New York, 1917, *The French Regime in Wisconsin and the Northwest,* New York, 1925; Henry C. Campbell, *Wisconsin in Three Centuries,* New York, 1906; H. E. Chambers, *History of Louisiana,* New York, 1925; Pierre F. X. de Charlevoix, *History . . . of New France,* 6 vols., New York, 1866; Agnes Laut, *Conquest of the Great Northwest,* New York, 1908; H. A. Innes, *The Fur Trade in Canada,* New Haven, 1930; Frederick W. Hodge and Charles F. Lummis, eds., *Memorial of Fray Alonzo de Benavides,* 1630, Chicago, 1916; Louis Hennepin, *New Discovery of a Vast Country in America,* 2 vols., Chicago, 1903; Isaac J. Cox, *Early Explorations of Louisiana,* Cincinnati, 1906; Consul W. Butterfield, *History of Discovery of the Northwest by John Nicolet in 1634,* Cincinnati, 1881; Frederick E. Gagnon, *Louis Jolliet,* Quebec, 1902.

as Europeans and extremely handsome. These were the Mandans, and near them were red people, the Arikaras, and in the same vast country dwelt a great nation of nomads which had for many years been visited by itinerant unidentified *voyageurs* – the Sioux. Men had found their way out to the plains rivers from the Missouri for several hundred miles, and some had gone on to Spanish territory.

It was known early that the great barrier of the mountains stood up beyond the buffalo plains, but the old dream of finding a water passage to the western sea could not be killed. Among those in whom it burned was the great pathfinder and trader, Pierre Gaultier de Varennes, Sieur de la Verendrye. One day, in 1726, he listened to an old Indian beside a campfide at Nipigon. The aged one illustrated his words with a crude map drawn on the ground. The map showed a broad river running straight into the ocean that lay beyond the big mountains.[6]

La Verendrye's blood raced. He could not go himself – he was unwell and too busy with trading problems – but he never ceased to dream of going. At last, in 1742, he sent his two sons, Francois and Louis Joseph, to find the western river.

They went first to the Mandan Villages, well known places now, and then set out west and southwest. They

---

[6] Lawrence J. Burpee, *Search for the Western Sea*, Toronto, 1908, and ed., *Journals and Letters of Pierre Gaultier do Varennes de la Verendrye*, Toronto, 1927; Arthur S. Morton, "La Verendrye" in *Canadian Historical Review*, 1928, no. 4; Doane Robinson, "La Verendrye's Farthest West," in *Proceedings*, State Historical Society of Wisconsin, 1913; J. W. Smurr, "A New La Verendrye Theory" in *Pacific Northwest Quarterly*, Jan. 1952; Charles E. Deland, "The Verendrye Explorations and Discoveries" in *South Dakota Historical Collections*, vol. 7, 1914.

found the Little Missouri, and they passed through the Badlands, and they crossed the Powder, and on January 1, 1742, they saw far to the west a great range of mountains – the Bighorns.

There, for reasons they did not adequately explain, they turned back, crossed the Belle Fouche, circled the Black Hills, and reached the Arikara village of Little Cherries on the Missouri. In a hillside they buried a metal plate to record their passage.[7]

A small gate had been opened, but it was not to be found by others for many years, and the country beyond the Bighorns was not to be seen until the American Mountain Men went beyond the old paths of the French and the British who had preceded them, and in time reached unknown regions on erratic expeditions.

The old pattern was to continue – the Indians had heard, if they had not yet seen, what the white man could produce and had to offer them – and not until the Mountain Men had pushed clear across the plains and mountains, taking trade goods within the reach of all tribes, would the centuries-old system be changed. Even then the change would be in the guise of a transfer of advantage, not the substitution of a new system. Then no Indians would be in a good position to gouge and defraud others. That privilege would be reserved exclusively for the white traders, and they would overlook no opportunity to benefit from it.

---

[7] At Pierre, South Dakota. The plate was found by a schoolgirl in 1913. Pierre was not named after either Verendrye, *pere ou fils,* but took its name from an American Fur Company trading post which was built in 1831, three miles above the mouth of the Teton River, and christened Fort Pierre in 1832 in honor of Pierre Chouteau.

Few trails were created by either the *voyageurs* or the Mountain Men. They found them, but the paths themselves had long been there, awaiting their coming.

The forces of nature, molding the contours of the earth, the lakes, the streams, the mountains, plains and deserts, had laid them out. The animals knew them and used them, and the first men followed the spoor of the animals.

The lines of least resistance guided the original traces and paths and highways. For the most part, these were water courses, and even though the Mountain Men established short cuts across prairies and hills, these, too, were influenced by the ways of the streams.

The Missouri was the great trunk highway east of the mountains, a natural thoroughfare into which poured the waters of a thousand tributaries, large and small. This system drained a watershed in excess of 500,000 square miles.[8]

On the Pacific slope were two great systems, the Colorado and the Columbia, but the Missouri was navigable within a comparatively short distance from its source, and the two largest rivers draining into the western sea were swift and frequently interrupted by great rapids and falls. They might form natural passages through the country, but, except in their lower reaches, they were unusable for transport.

No more than a decade after the return of Lewis and Clark, the Mountain Men had made discoveries which clearly established the natural characteristics of the

---

[8] Nearly the equivalent of the present huge state of Alaska (571,000 sq. mi.), or almost double the area of the state of Texas.

American West's interior. They knew that if a circle
with a diameter of one hundred miles were drawn
around the Grand Teton its circumference would en-
compass headwaters of all three great western river systems, the Missouri, the Colorado and the Columbia.
Within it were sources of the waters which united at
the Three Forks to form the Missouri, and the sources
of the Snake, which was the southern branch of the
Columbia, and sources of the Green, the main tributary
of the Colorado. Moreover, water rising in the circle
contributed to other important streams – the Yellowstone,
the Wind, the Big Horn.

This was the fountainhead of the West, a land of unsurpassed majesty and grandeur, its great peaks tumbled
against the sky, its forests sweeping up from clear tur-
quoise lakes, a land of deep valleys and towering ridges,
awesome chasms and thundering falls, alpine meadow-
lands and glaciers and hot springs, the heart of the western wilderness and wrapped in its pressing silence.

Of all the rivers emptying into the Missouri, the
Yellowstone and the Platte were the most important –
although not for the same reasons – to the Mountain Men.

The Platte was regarded as the dividing line between
the upper and lower basins of the Missouri. It was a
conception which had no basis in geography, for the
main Missouri was three times longer above than it was
below the Platte's mouth, and there were no physical
features, such as a high range, which might have created
a natural division of the two areas. Yet, the *voyageurs*
and the Mountain Men marked the passage of the Platte
in a way similar to that of sailors who crossed the
Equator, that is, with festivities.

The reason was to be found in what the Platte was, what it meant and what it represented. The Platte was, like the Missouri and the Yellowstone, one of the gateways to the Far West. After one passed it, ascending the river, the next good thoroughfare to the mountains was the Yellowstone, more than twelve hundred miles ahead. Numerous streams entered the Missouri between the Platte and the Yellowstone, but they were of small consequence, and they proffered no feasible through route.

The Platte was a thousand miles long, and it ran for most of this distance through plains country. It was wide and shallow, seldom navigable even in canoes or with rafts, and its bed was composed largely of fine sand which was constantly shifted by the current, so that no permanent channel was carved, as would have been the case had it flowed through harder material.

A few miles east of the 101st meridian, on the steadily rising short grass plains, the Platte divided. The sources of both the north and south branches were among the high peaks of the Shining Mountains, but the waters reached their junction by widely divergent routes. The North Platte flowed northward several hundred miles, picking up the Sweetwater and the Laramie rivers. The South Platte's course was generally eastward, but upon escaping the mountains it turned northward along their eastern base, then northeastward to the main stream. Both forks provided comparatively easy access routes to the mountain country.

If the Mountain Men could not travel on the Platte, they could travel beside it. From each bank reached away an ocean of buffalo grass. Game in the valley of the Platte was usually plentiful, and there, too, numerous tribes hunted and followed war trails, and some dwelt permanently beside the life-giving waters.

The Yellowstone was the largest of all rivers that joined the Missouri. Indians said of it that it came out of a land which the Manitous who had created the earth had not yet completed. Carrying its great foaming burden, the Yellowstone followed a northerly course over falls and rapids and through immense canyons for 150 miles, then turned east and sped down the eastern slope of the mountains to the northern plains, whence it swung gradually to the northeast and its meeting with the Missouri, almost exactly on the 104th meridian at 48 degrees north latitude.[9]

It and its major tributaries—Clark's Fork, Big Horn, Tongue, Powder—were doors to an enormous country on the eastern side of the Continental Divide, and in ascending the Yellowstone, if the Mountain Men left it where its course turned sharply southward and traversed the few miles of a pass, they might reach the Madison, Jefferson and Gallatin Rivers at the Three Forks of the Missouri. The Three Forks country was one of the richest fur-producing areas in all the West.

The mountain ranges and the hills were barriers, the rivers were gateways. Moreover, in the stream valleys the Mountain Men found the resources they must have to survive. There were the best grazing grounds, therefore the most game of all kinds. There were groves which

---

[9] See Webb, *op. cit.;* Billington, *op. cit.;* Hiram M. Chittenden, *History of the American Fur Trade of the Far West,* 3 vols., New York, 1902, and reprinted 1935 and 1954; Thomas Hart Benton, *Thirty Years' View,* Boston, 1854.

supplied fuel and shelter. There were fish and great flocks of wildfowls – ducks, geese, turkeys and prairie chickens, swans and cranes, quail and grouse.

From the time of man's first coming, the valleys were the routes of migration, and they sustained him. They were the routes of commerce and war. It was that way when the Mountain Men arrived. The tribes were in the valleys because the buffalo were on the plains bordering the streams, and the wild fruits and roots and herbs were there. Everything the Mountain Men needed was there for them, just as it had been for the Indians.

There was another important reason for following the rivers and creeks. The beaver, the most wanted of all furs, lived in them. This circumstance made even more enticing and profitable the happy combination of natural resources and feasible routes of transport and trade.

History was made on the streams, big and little, and most of it was made where they came together. Mark out only the main confluences, and you are marking out the sites of the most vital and significant events – commercial, military, social, political – which transpired since man first walked the western earth.

The confluences were crossroads. There were joined the paths of people now lost in the impenetrable shadows of timeless antiquity. There the hunting and trading trails of later tribes that lived within the span of recorded history – for example, the Crow, Sioux, Blackfeet, Ute, Bannock, Flathead, Cheyenne, Arapahoe, Shoshone, Nez Perce, Pawnees, Kiowa – met and ran on into the sky in each direction.

These were the same paths used by the Mountain Men, and by the caravans of later fur traders. They were the trails that felt the weight of the first wheels to creak across the seas of grass to the mountains, writing sagas with the ruts they left in their wakes. The Dragoons and the cavalry and the foot-soldiers followed them through all the terrible years of the western campaigns, and over them snaked the long wagon trains, marking with their refuse the end of one era and the beginning of another.

At the confluences were the best views of the pageant of the Far West, an unending parade of dreams and hopes and realities and conflicts. The voices of the righteous and of the damned were heard in the cottonwood trees that shaded the banks. The cries of the warriors were interspersed with the howls of the wolves. The calls of the sick and of the wounded were lost in the silence of the stars, and the moon gave shadows to the shrouds of the dead.

Laughter rang out about the campfires, and flesh rotted with disease, and women groaned in the agony of giving new lives to the eternal cycle. Old men dreamed there with sad hearts of the greatness they once had known and which would not come again to them, and deep drums gave rhythm to savage manifestations, and bugles sang of a new day and a new way that had come upon the West.

The time came, America's time, when out of the East emerged a breed of men who brought miraculous tools and weapons that met in deadly combat with the tools and weapons of their primitive brothers. The invaders came with flying banners that signified a new kind of God and a new kind of life. The symbols and crafts of Christianity and civilization clashed with the eagle feathers and the medicine bag – emblems and instruments which could not possibly exist together in compatibility and peace.

The shaping of the earth created the confluences, but it was man, seeking, as he had done from his beginning, beneficial geographical characteristics, who made *rendezvous* of them. And to them man brought all his troubles, all his controversies, the petty and the important, all his curses and ideals, his wickedness and goodness, his vices and his virtues, his sacrilege and his reverence. He made of them crossroads of his existence, not only of his passages from place to place, but of his fancies and schemings, persuasions and tenets – all products which, if they were in themselves mysterious and inexplicable, inevitably fomented dissension and misunderstanding.

So man gave to these meeting places of the wilderness waters identities that were significant and indestructible, irremovable from his story.

No one had known the exact size of Louisiana Territory. The best Napoleon's ministers could do was to state that France was selling to the United States the same amount of the North American Continent it had ceded to Spain in 1762 and had taken back from Spain in 1802. There was no mention of exact boundaries. These would be delineated in time, but not before the Mountain Men had penetrated into virtually every nook and cranny of the vast land mass.

It would come to be determined that Louisiana Territory contained 909,130 square miles, 581,843,200 acres.

The cost to the United States had been $15,000,000, or
.0257 cents an acre.

No one, least of all the officials of the two nations,
had any idea how many Indians lived in the territory,
but it was believed that in 1802 about 44,000 white
and Negro persons and mulattoes could be found there.
The great majority of these people, possessing more than
three-quarters of the total wealth, lived in the area of
the lower Mississippi.

Congress, in its unexplained wisdom, saw fit to divide
the immense acquisition at the thirty-third parallel.[10]
The area south of this arbitrary line was to be called
the Territory of Orleans. The area north of it (more
than 18 times as large) was named the District of Louisiana, and for administrative purposes it was temporarily
placed under the jurisdiction of Indiana Territory.

Not only did no one know how large the District of
Louisiana was, or what it contained, or exactly where its
boundaries were, but the number of non-Indian persons
in it was as undetermined, and as undeterminable, as
the number of Indians. The best guess, furnished by
vague Spanish officials, was seven thousand whites, mulattoes, Negro slaves and free Negroes – about one person
for every 78,000 square miles.

Of course, nearly all of the seven thousand lived in
the town of St. Louis, and in adjacent settlements and
villages lower down the Mississippi.

It was in the spring of 1764 that the noise of hammer-
ing and sawing broke the wilderness silence on a bench
land above the Mississippi River, just a short distance

---

[10]Approximately the boundary between the states of Arkansas and Louisiana.

below the mouth of the Missouri. Pierre Laclede Liguest and thirty men, nearly all of whom were craftsmen, were building the settlement they had named St. Louis in honor of the patron saint of their king, Louis xv. They had come up the river from New Orleans the previous fall and had spent the winter at Fort Chartres. Maxent, Laclede & Company had been given a grant for the exclusive fur trade of the Missouri River and of the upper Mississippi, but in the time it had taken Laclede and his men to travel by keelboat upstream to Fort Chartres, the grant had been made legally worthless by the transfer of Louisiana Territory from France to Spain.

Laclede went ahead with his plan. In the group was a young man of fourteen, Auguste Chouteau, whom Laclede considered an able and trustworthy assistant. Chouteau was given the duty of overseeing the construction work and of making sure that the plan for the village which Laclede had drawn was followed. Trading with the Indians was soon begun, and once again young Chouteau was in the forefront. He would, when he found the time propitious, launch the famous trading dynasty that would play a dominant role in the western fur trade for more than a century.

The Spanish took over in due course, but the French traders had little difficulty in operating under most of the governors who held office during the next forty years, a situation rarely found, if at all, in the annals of Spanish colonies of the Western Hemisphere.

The original traders formed partnerships and reached agreements among the native tribes. In the main, they respected each other's claims. Their numbers increased, and competition developed, but expansion was always possible, and the trade routes were pushed steadily farther into the wilderness, which began at the edge of the village.

Families were brought from New Orleans, even from the West Indies and from Europe, and with them came the culture and the manner of living which they had known in their ancestral homes. Spacious residences rose among wide gardens and grounds shaded by great trees. Slaves polished carriages, groomed good horses, shined brass door plates, kept log fires burning in handsomely furnished rooms, and silver flatware caught the light of candles on dinner tables covered with imported linens.

Good taste, affluence and prosperity, however, were found in only a small part of St. Louis. Its grubbiness increased commensurately with its rapid growth, and by 1800 it presented a ragged cluster of clapboard, stone, log and earthen buildings, a conglomeration of shacks, hovels, cabins, dilapidated shops and dwellings edging the graceful, well-tended residences set appropriately back from the noisy commerce of *La Rue Royale* and *La Rue de la Tour*.[11]

For more than a score of years the leading St. Louis traders—such men as the Chouteaus, Gratiots, Cerres, Benoits, Gregoires, Sarpys, Sanguinets, and the dynamic Spaniard, Manuel Lisa—had not shown more than a casual interest in the far northern country. They had left it to the British, being satisfied with conditions and the amount of trade obtainable much nearer home. They had always made good money among the tribes of the lower Missouri, the Illinois, and even as far south as the Arkansas, and west for some distance on the Kansas

---

[11] Later, respectively, Main and Walnut streets.

and the Platte . . . the Missouris, Otoes, Kansas, Omahas, Pawnees, Arapahoes, Sac, Foxes, Illinois, Iowas, Osages.

The predominate language of St. Louis, and particularly in the fur trade, was French. This was not due to the influence of the prominent families, but to the bulk of the population which, as the eighteenth century neared an end, had come from the old towns of Vincennes, Cahokia, Kaskaskia and Fort de Chartres. From Canada had come the *voyageurs,* many of them of mixed bloods, but all of whom spoke French.

The St. Louisans did not share the extreme ideas of the motherland revolutionists. They preferred the quiet, easier ways of their forefathers. Political innovations and modern social theories had no attraction for them. In dealings among themselves they were honest and punctilious, so that they had little need for courts or lawyers. Dealing with Indians was, of course, another matter. Trading was trading, and the sharpest men deserved the victories. They were cruel and unsympathetic in their relations with the people upon whom they depended for their living.

Suddenly, seemingly almost overnight, the way of life St. Louis had known and enjoyed for so long was changed. Louisiana was sold to the United States. The old residents wept as the standard of the French Republique was supplanted by the Stars and Stripes, but there was nothing they could do about the matter. Like it or not, they were Americans.

This fact was quickly made apparent to them in other, and less gentle, ways. Across the Mississippi poured a heterogeneous parade, accompanied by a lasting uproar.

American traders and merchants, hunters from Virginia, Kentucky and Tennessee, river louts, boat hands, prostitutes, soldiers and government officials, gamblers and thieves, degenerates and false prophets crowded the streets. As if by magic appeared brothels, saloons, cafes, shops and inns, trading emporiums and all manner of ramshackle establishments, some of them no more than holes dug in the bank of the river.[12]

The upper Missouri, so long dominated by British traders, was American territory. Foreigners would have no rights there. This was the land of the Sioux, of the Grosventres, the Crows, the Assinibiones, the Blackfeet, and it was a land rich in furs.

Moreover, there was nothing to stop newcomers from invading the lower river territories which the old St. Louis trading families had had for more than two generations almost entirely to themselves.

The St. Louis traders began to think and move with speed and energy to which they had never been accustomed.

---

[12]The population of the area that was to become Missouri Territory was probably no more than 4,000 in 1803. The extent of the influx which took place in the years immediately following the Louisiana Purchase may be judged from the size of the population of the territory in 1820; that year the U.S. Census reported it as 66,586. Few efforts were made to enumerate Negro slaves, Indians or persons of mixed blood, of which there were many. See Albert Richardson, *Beyond the Mississippi,* Hartford, 1867; Robert Riegel, *America Moves West,* New York, 1930, and revised reprints; Frederick L. Paxson, *History of the American Frontier,* New York, 1924; David Lavender, *Westward Vision,* New York, 1963; Donald C. Peattie, *Forward the Nation,* New York, 1942; Cardinal Goodwin, *The Trans-Mississippi West,* New York, 1922; W. J. Ghent, *The Early Far West,* New York, 1931; Dan E. Clark, *The West in American History,* New York, 1937; Henry M. Brackenridge, *Views of Louisiana,* Pittsburg, 1814; Everett Dick, *Vanguards of the Frontier,* New York, 1941; James Hall, *Statistics of the West,* Cincinnati, 1836; Louis Houck, *History of Missouri,* 3 vols., New York, 1908.

President Jefferson tried to obtain some maps of the eastern part of Louisiana Territory. There were none, at least none on paper. The only maps in existence were in the heads of *voyageurs,* both Creoles and Canadians, who had gone into the wilderness west of the Mississippi. When one of them died, or was killed by animals or Indians, his map died with him.

Mr. Jefferson's dream of exploring the Far West had not been born with the Louisiana purchase. Before that he had proposed sending out expeditions ostensibly to conduct scientific observations, but the Spanish had not been cooperative. Scientific expeditions had a way of turning into military incursions.

This problem was eliminated, at least in theory, by the purchase, but for some time the Spanish refused to recognize the legality of the deal between France and America, and Americans were obliged to obtain Spanish passports to enter American territory.

With Lewis and Clark on their way up the Missouri, Mr. Jefferson turned to plans he had in mind for exploring and surveying other areas. He asked Congress for funds, but Congress appeared to be still somewhat dazed by the magnitude of the Louisiana transaction and the political and administrative problems it presented. Scientific studies could be undertaken in good time. After all, one company already was wandering somewhere on the upper Missouri, and no one had heard a word from it. Prudence dictated slowness in such fields. The sum of $3,000 was all Congress was willing to appropriate in response to the President's request. It was hardly enough for even a small expedition.

But Mr. Jefferson went ahead, and late in 1804 he

got William Dunbar, a scientist living in Mississippi Territory, and George Hunter, a Philadelphia chemist, to start with a little company of seventeen men up the Red River. This was country the Spanish still claimed, and from Chihuahua came orders that no American was to be permitted to approach the Texas frontier.

Under the circumstances, the Dunbar-Hunter Expedition decided that the Ouachita River was more suitable for exploration, and turned up it. Instead of a completely unknown and empty wilderness they came upon several settlements of French-Canadian, Spanish and Creole families, and even a few German, Irish and American settlers. Some of these people had lived out there for more than a generation. They weren't botanists, surveyors or zoologists, but they could tell any scientist a thing or two about the flora and fauna and the contours of the country. Somewhat more surprising to the expedition was the "discovery" that at Fort Miro, about two hundred miles up the river, was an American military detachment and some 150 families of civilians. Dunbar and Hunter poked around, bathed in some large hot springs, and turned back. Their trip took a little more than three months.[13]

General James Wilkinson of the American Army became the first governor of Louisiana Territory in 1805. He was at the time a paid spy of the Spanish government, a participant in Aaron Burr's conspiracy, a corrupt public official, and a dishonest businessman.

President Jefferson's desire to have the upper Missis-

---

[13] Hot Springs, Arkansas. See Billington, *op. cit.*; Ghent, *op. cit.*; Charles E. A. Gayarre, *History of Louisiana,* New York, 1854-66, reprinted New Orleans, 1879, 1885, 1903.

sippi country explored was not an official secret, and Wilkinson, in the hope of augmenting his own prestige and gaining some glory for himself, organized an expedition without authority. It was not without careful thought that he selected an unknown and highly ineligible young lieutenant named Zebulon Montgomery Pike to head it. Plans extremely unfavorable to his own government were already revolving in Wilkinson's mind, and Pike was a likely candidate for a role in them.

Pike took his company up the Mississippi and selected Lake Leech as its source, an error that was soon to be rectified. He held several councils with Indians who listened to him but made no important commitments. His scientific observations were inaccurate. The total worth of his accomplishments, in fact, amounted to little, but Wilkinson was not concerned with what Pike had done as much as he was with what Pike might do in connection with his own nefarious schemes.

Having squeezed another $5,000 from Congress, President Jefferson launched a second attempt to have the Red River explored to its source, and he selected Thomas Freeman, an amateur surveyor and astronomer, to undertake the task. After lengthy negotiations with Spanish officials, Freeman got off in April, 1806. Ascending the river with great difficulty for about six hundred miles, he was stopped by a Spanish military force, and turned back. Nothing was accomplished, and, like Dunbar and Hunter, Freeman found that French *voyageurs* had preceded him and were thoroughly familiar with the country he had reached.

Zebulon Montgomery Pike had been back in St. Louis less than three months from his Mississippi venture when

Wilkinson dispatched him on the trail west with an expedition which allegedly had for its purpose the exploration of the sources of both the Red and Arkansas rivers. It was also to treat with Indians in those areas. This was a well calculated deception. Pike was a spy for Wilkinson, who was studiously engaged in advancing the intrigues devised by Burr.[14]

Pike was secretly instructed to conduct a military reconnaissance of Spanish territory. It was a maneuver which logically would have been taken by men conspiring to conquer a foreign possession with force of arms and establish a new nation. Winkinson was using his high rank as commander of the army in Louisiana Territory to further his own traitorous designs. Neither the President nor the War Department had any inkling of his machinations. If Pike had no knowledge of them, as he was to maintain, he was a loyal subordinate willing to carry out orders to spy on a neighboring power with which his country was, at least officially, at peace.

A civilian whom Pike was ordered to take with him, however, was fully apprised of the Burr-Wilkinson plot. He was Dr. James Hamilton Robinson. It was announced that the expedition would have the advantages of Dr. Robinson's medical services, but Dr. Robinson's secret orders were to enter Santa Fe, and there, under the pretext of attempting to collect a bill due a St. Louis trader, observe the strength of the Spanish forces and obtain other information which might be of value to an invader.

---

[14]See Zebulon M. Pike, *Account of Expeditions to the Sources of the Mississippi and through Western Parts of Louisiana,* Philadelphia, 1810, or the edition edited by Elliott Coues, 3 vols., New York, 1895, reprinted Minneapolis, 1965; *Zebulon Pike's Arkansas Journal,* ed. by Stephen H. Hart and A. B. Hulbert, Colorado Springs, 1932.

There were only twenty-three men in the company. Pike traveled across the plains, passing the site of a trading post, Fort Carondelet, which Auguste Chouteau had built in 1794. He met with French traders and learned that his trail had already been traversed by them clear to the western mountains. He ascended the Arkansas, and on a favorable site in the afternoon shadows of the great snow-covered ranges, he built a stockade.[15]

His efforts to climb an immense peak, which was named for him, ended in failure. In the dead of winter he crossed the Sangre de Cristo Range, reached a small tributary of the Rio Grande, and erected another stockade. A few days later, Dr. Robinson set off on his mission to Santa Fe.

Spanish spies in St. Louis had suspected Wilkinson and saw a plot in the making to seize New Mexico. They sent messengers with this intelligence to the provincial governor. On February 26, 1807, Spanish dragoons appeared at the stockade on Conejos Creek, took Pike and his men prisoners, and marched them off to the New Mexican capital, whence they were sent to Chihuahua. In vain did Pike protest that he had not known he was on the west side of the Rio Grande, but thought he had reached the headwaters of the Red River.

Four months later the expedition was escorted out of Spanish territory and delivered to American authorities at Natchitoches. In the sense that Pike brought back the first reliable information concerning military, commercial and political situations in the Spanish provinces, the expedition had some value. In every other respect it was a failure.

---

[15] Pueblo, Colorado.

With one notable exception, the first American expeditions to explore Louisiana Territory had been largely unsuccessful, but the single exception had given brilliant reality to Thomas Jefferson's dream.

The journey of Lewis and Clark had been an unqualified success, an accomplishment that fired the blood of all Americans, an heroic feat which sent national pride soaring to an unprecedented height. Not without sound reasons would it be seen by future generations . . . long after all the western wilderness had been conquered . . . as the most perfect achievement of its kind in all the world's history.

St. Louis was the hive. The richest honey was a thousand miles, two thousand and even farther, away, but the bees were after it. The Mountain Men had gone out.

A rare kind of men, they would never number more than a few hundred, and they would become extinct with greater rapidity than they had been created.[16]

---

[16] Histories of the American fur trade and of the men who are engaged in it are legion. No attempt will be made here to present a comprehensive bibliography of these works. Rather it is my intention to guide the interested student to sources which will provide a general knowledge of this most fascinating era. An excellent starting point is Hiram A. Chittenden's *History of the American Fur Trade of the Far West,* cited above. A reliable history of the fur trade, from its beginning in Canada to the end of the American period, is Paul C. Phillips' *The Fur Trade,* Norman, Okla., 1961. From these two launching pads one may fly in many directions. Works pertaining to the Ashley period will be cited in Part 5 herein. A fund of information on the fur trade, its general history and accounts of specific events, may be obtained from the following. Hubert H. Bancroft, *History of Washington, Idaho and Montana,* San Francisco, 1890; Albert L. Belden, *The Fur Trade of America,* New York, 1917; William M. Anderson, *Anderson's Narrative of a Ride to the Rocky Mountains in 1834,* Missoula, 1938; Frederick L. Billon, *Annals of St. Louis in its Early Days,* 2 vols.,

If there was a common strain in the Mountain Men, it stemmed not from nationality, not from teaching, not from environment, not from religious beliefs, nor from any economic, social or political condition. They came from too many different places, from too many contrasting situations, too many walks of life, for that. It stemmed from a combination of natural elements, a

St. Louis, 1886-88; John J. Audubon, *Audubon and His Journals,* New York, 1897; Alpheus H. Favour, *Old Bill Williams,* Chapel Hill, No. Car., 1936; Gordon C. Davidson, *The North West Company,* Berkeley, 1918; A. S. Doughty and C. Martin, eds., *The Kelsey Papers,* Ottawa, 1929; Harlin M. Fuller and L. R. Hafen, eds., *Journal of John R. Bell of S. H. Long Expedition,* Glendale, Calif., 1957; Victor R. Fuchs, *Economics of the Fur Industry,* New York, 1957; M. M. Backus, *Fur and the Fur Trade,* Boston, 1879; John Ball, *Autobiography,* Glendale, Calif., 1925; Blanche C. Grant, *When Old Trails Were New,* New York, 1934; LeRoy R. and Ann W. Hafen, eds., *To the Rockies and Oregon,* 1839-42, Glendale, Calif., 1955; Hubert H. Bancroft, *History of Nevada, Colorado and Wyoming,* San Francisco, 1890; Benjamin F. Gue, *History of Iowa,* 4 vols., New York, 1903; Edwin James, *Account of an Expedition from Pittsburgh to the Rocky Mountains . . . 1819-20,* Philadelphia, 1823, and Cleveland, 1905; I. S. Bartlett, *History of Wyoming,* 3 vols., Chicago, 1918; C. N. Bell, ed., *Journal of Henry Kelsey,* Winnipeg, 1929; Peter Skene Ogden, *Snake Country Journals,* ed by E. E. Rich, London, 1950; John Bradbury, *Travels in the Interior of America,* Liverpool, 1817, and Cleveland, 1904; Medorem Crawford, *Journal,* Eugene, Oreg., 1897; William M. Darlington, *Christopher Gist's Journals,* New York, 1893; F. A. Chardon, *Journal at Fort Clark,* Pierre, 1932; Frederick J. Turner, *Character and Influence of Indian Trade in Wisconsin: a study of trading posts,* Baltimore, 1891; Carl I. Wheat, *Mapping the Trans-Mississippi West,* 2 vols., San Francisco, 1958; William S. Wallace, *Antoine Robidoux,* Los Angeles, 1953; Dorothy Gardner, *West of the River,* New York, 1940; Bernard DeVoto, *Across the Wide Missouri,* Boston, 1947; Warren Ferris, *Life in the Rocky Mountains,* Denver, 1940; Thomas J. Farnham, *Travels in the Great Western Prairies,* Poughkeepsie, 1841, London, 1843, Cleveland, 1906; Frederick Dellenbaugh, *Breaking the Wilderness,* New York, 1905; Samuel Hancock, *Narrative,* New York, 1927; Edward Harris, *Up the Missouri with Audubon,* Norman, Okla., 1951; Grace, R. Hebard, *Pathbreakers from River to Ocean,* Chicago, 1911, and revised reprints; Washington Irving, *Adventures of Captain Bonneville,* New York, 1847, frequent reprints; Sidney Greenbie, *Frontiers and the Fur Trade,* New York, 1929; L. R. Hafen and W. J.

chemical formula, that was as unique as its compounding was inexplicable. The true Mountain Man was born, a product of the mysterious forces which give character and identity to every living organism, every body and brain and bone and sinew. He was developed and trained through experience and action, but he was not made by them.

Ghent, *Broken Hand: Thomas Fitzpatrick*, Denver, 1931; William Hamilton, *My Sixty Years on the Plains*, New York, 1905, and reprints; Charles Larpenteur, *Forty Years a Fur Trader on the Upper Missouri*, ed. by Coues, New York, 1898, Minneapolis, 1962, and ed. Quaife, Chicago, 1933; Zenas Leonard, *Narrative of Adventures*, Clearfield, Pa., 1839, and later reprints; John C. Luttig, *Journal of a Fur Trading Expedition on the Upper Missouri*, St. Louis, 1920; Alexander Majors, *Seventy Years on the Frontier*, New York, 1893; John K. Townsend, *Narrative of a Journey across the Rocky Mountains*, Philadelphia, 1839; Maximilian, Prince of Wied, *Travels in the Interior of North America*, London, 1843, and Cleveland, 1906; H. M. Chittenden and A. T. Richardson, *Life, Letters and Travels of Father Pierre-Jean de Smet, S. J.*, 4 vols., New York, 1905; Nolie Mumey, *Life of Jim Baker*, Denver, 1931; George Nidever, *Life and Adventures*, ed. by W. H. Ellison, Berkeley, 1937; Osborne Russell, *Journal of a Trapper*, Boise, 1914, and Portland, Oreg., 1955; Samuel Parker, *Journal of an Exploring Tour beyond the Rocky Mountains*, Ithaca, 1838; Rufus R. Wilson, *Out of the West*, New York, 1936; George F. Ruxton, *Adventures in Mexico and the Rocky Mountains*, London, 1847, and *Life in the Far West*, Edinburgh, 1849; Clyde and Mae R. Porter, *Ruxton of the Rockies*, Norman, Okla., 1950; Rufus B. Sage, *Scenes in the Rocky Mountains*, Philadelphia, 1846, and reprinted with his letters and papers, ed. by L. R. and Ann W. Hafen, Glendale, Calif., 1956; John Upton Terrell, *Furs by Astor*, New York, 1963, and *Black Robe* (DeSmet), New York, 1964; Stephen Hall Meek, *Autobiography*, Pasadena, 1948; Andrew Jackson, "Message from the President concerning the Fur Trade," in *Sen. Exec. Doc. no. 90*, 22 Cong., 1 sess., Washington, 1832; Rudolph F. Kurz, *Journal*, Washington, Bur. of Am. Ethnol., 1937; William Kelly, *Across the Rocky Mountains*, London, 1852; F. A. Wislizenus, *Journey to the Rocky Mountains in 1839*, St. Louis, 1912; J. F. Kinney, *Career of Henry Kelsey*, Ottawa, 1929; John Work, *Journal*, Cleveland, 1923; Robert G. Cleland, *This Reckless Breed of Men*, New York, 1950; Edwin Bryant, *Rocky Mountain Adventures*, New York, 1885, a reprint of his *What I Saw in California*, 1848; LeRoy R. Hafen, ed., *The Mountain Men and the Fur Trade of the Far West*, Glendale, Calif., 1965-68 (six vols. issued to date; biographies).

Like any other separable, identifiable group or kind, the mark of the gentleman was on some of them, as was the mark of the inferior. Among them were the vulgar and the decent, the cruel and the kind, the filthy and the clean, the large and the small, the handsome and the ugly, the affectionate and the cold, the honest and the deceitful, the infidel and the devout. They were all the things that men are, yet they stood apart, for they had something more than the commonplace qualities, both admirable and execrable, of their blood brothers.

The Mountain Man who survived for any length of time after crossing the frontier possessed a native shrewdness and sensitivity that were as infrequently found as winter primroses on the plains. These were the indestructible rocks upon which the structure of his nature stood, the scaffolding which contained no substances existing in the weak, the stupid, the fool, the timid, the visionary, but only those materials which gave being and definition to the courageous, the stoical, the strong, the obdurate.

The Mountain Man who came back was the one who had the cunning, viciousness, heart, stealth and stamina of the animals, and the distrust, understanding and wilderness knowledge of the Indian, among both of which he was obliged to live and with which he must continually combat. Without these things he did not come back, and often, although he had them, they were not enough.

The West was bigger and more powerful than any man, and it had a way of impartially eliminating some of the best and some of the worst, as if to remind all who ventured into it that it, and it alone, was the supreme master of their destiny.

The Mountain Men were going out, and the writing of national epics had begun. It was the spring of 1807. Lewis and Clark were in the East, still reporting and being honored.

The journals they had so conscientiously kept had been seen by only a few people, but word of mouth accounts, opinions and views from them and from their men had traveled swiftly across the land. Many statements they had not uttered were attributed to them. They were given credit for discovering things they had not even dreamed about, or which didn't exist.

It was not their descriptions of the country, not the geography they had noted, not the weather observations they had made, not the tribes they encountered, that excited St. Louis. All these things were interesting and good to know about, but it was what they said the country contained that made the blood of St. Louis race. They talked of mountain streams swarming with beaver, of an almost inconceivable wealth of all species of furbearing animals. That was what spurred to action the old traders and the young, the newcomers who were drifting across the Mississippi with their long rifles and coonskin caps from the eastern woodlands and mountains, and the men who had come much greater distances, who had burrs in their tongues – wanderers and adventurers all. History would not forget some of them.

In New York, a prime beaver skin was worth $6 to $8. Otter would sell at $4 to $5. Buffalo robes brought $4, and deer skins 30 cents a pound. Even a muskrat skin would bring 30 to 40 cents. Shipments went straight through to the east coast now without border troubles. It was all one country, with one government. Fortunes were waiting takers on the upper rivers, waiting the first to reach them.

The big keelboats being loaded were products of an evolution that was colored by bitter experience and the blood of the rivermen who had devised them. They were fifty to seventy-five feet long, fifteen to eighteen feet in width, drew three or four feet of water, and had a heavy keel running from bow to stern. The cargo hold was amidships, a deck ten or twelve feet in length at each end of it. In some boats the freight space had been sacrificed to cabins in which prominent passengers could be quartered.

The chief means of propulsion was the *cordelle,* a long line attached to the top of a mast so that it would clear shore brush. On the bank, twenty to forty men toiled with it over their shoulders. When the *cordelle* could not be operated because of stream mouths or high cliffs, poles would be used. The poles had knobs on their upper ends, and these would be placed under the shoulders of the pushers. Planting his pole on the river bottom, a *voyageur* would push against it as he walked toward the stern along the *passe avant,* a passage only fifteen inches in width on each side of the cargo hold. In deep water, long oars would be brought out, and six or eight men seated on each side of the bow would bend their backs against them. Wide water and a favorable wind came at the same time now and then, permitting the use of a sail, and on these rare occasions the men would sprawl about, chatting, singing, laughing, enjoying the luxury of the brief respite.

An uninitiated person observing a departing keelboat might have thought it was carrying only a band of

Indians or wild halfbreeds. The heads of some of the hunters would be sheathed in handkerchief turbans. Others would still be wearing winter fur caps. Their shirts would be dressed deerskin and their buckskin breeches would be wrapped about their legs under the tops of moccasins. When spring blizzards struck they would don heavy hooded capotes. Almost everything they wore would be embroidered, fringed and ornamented with feathers and beads and colored hair work.

Some of the men going up the river carried long Kentucky rifles, which were made in Pennsylvania, but not much time was to pass before most of these would be supplanted by the gun designed specifically to meet the demands of the West . It would be shorter, and could be carried more conveniently on horseback, and it could be loaded and fired with greater facility. The gunmakers would call it the plains rifle.

Other hunters in that spring of 1807 carried the United States army flintlock model of 1803, which might kill a man at three hundred yards, but would only irritate a grizzly bear. And there would be other guns abroad, some of them of British manufacture, perhaps a blunderbuss or two with wide muzzles which discharged scattershot, and a few old muskets long outmoded but still revered and trusted by their owners.

Powder horns hung from shoulders as did leather straps to which were attached ammunition boxes and bags which contained a man's *possibles,* the few personal belongings he would take into the wilderness, such things as needles and thongs for repairing his clothing, a bit of soap, tobacco, perhaps a small Crucifix or Bible, a treasured letter, a few bright gewgaws which delighted his eye and would be worn on special occasions.

Two thousand miles of wild muddy current would lie ahead of a boat after it turned into the mouth of the Missouri. There would be weeks of backbreaking labor through storms, terrible heat, numbing cold, rain, snow and hail; weeks during which every hour would bring its perils, the treachery of the river, its boils and eddies, crumbling banks, snags and bars, animals and wilder savages who were even more unpredictable than the weather or the Missouri.

They would always be within the United States, but there would be no law, no civil or military authorities. If the government would be there in theory, it would not be there in reality. If laws had been written, they would be meaningless, for there would be no way of enforcing them.

On some far upper waterway they would build a post, and the only law, either there or in the surrounding wilderness, would be the *bourgeois,* the partner in the company. Yet, the *bourgeois* would provide little protection for the individual hunter, *voyageur* or *engage.* The *bourgeois,* holding supreme power, could act as he pleased or as he thought best. He could cast a man out, rob him of his wages with dishonest bookkeeping, shoot him. Or he could, if he so desired, be kind, considerate, fair. The *bourgeois'* first duty was to guard the company's investment. Furs were more important than men. Even horses ranked above them. The furs had to get back to St. Louis. The agreements signed by the men said they had to go out, but it was not stipulated that they had to come back.

Up there on the northern rivers, two or three thousand miles from the nearest church steeple and altar a man could not feel moved to place all his trust in God. There were too many manitous to be reckoned with. Divided power could give a man no reliable protection. It was better that a man looked to his own powers, his own resources, for no matter how great a man's faith he must recognize the cold reality of his situation: all that stood between him and an unmarked grave were his own superstitions, his own knowledge of ghosts, his own ability to sense danger in time, to smell it in the wind, see it in the markings of the dust, hear it in the whispers of the grass.

In that spring of 1807, Manuel Lisa's boat got away on April 19. It was the first major American trading expedition ever to start up the Missouri.

The company had no more than reached St. Charles, a short distance above the mouth, when it was overtaken by the acting governor, Frederick Bates, from whom Lisa had obtained his license to trade. Bates had good reasons for asking Lisa to delay his departure for a few days.

When Lewis and Clark had reached the Mandan Villages, on their way home, they had persuaded the chief, Gros Blanc, to accompany them to Washington, where he would be received by President Jefferson. Gros Blanc was assured that he and his interpreter, Rene Jesseaume, would be guarded at all times by soldiers, and their safe return was guaranteed. The chief's request that both he and the interpreter be permitted to take a wife and one child was granted. All expenses would be paid by the Great White Father.

A military escort of twenty-six men had been assigned

to escort Gros Blanc back to his home. It would travel with two other trading parties, and a deputation of Sioux which recently had come down the river to confer with government officials. Bates asked that Lisa wait until these contingents could join him, so that all might have greater protection on the long journey.

Lisa promised that he would delay his departure, but Bates had no sooner got out of sight than he started. He saw possible advantages in reaching the upper rivers ahead of the others. Startling plans, based more on hope than actual knowledge, had taken shape in his head, and he did not intend to have them interrupted by the encumbrance of competing traders.

Lisa's partners were William Morrison and Pierre Menard of Kaskaskia, but they were represented by George Drouillard, who had been with Lewis and Clark.[17] He could talk in the language of the hands, and few could surpass him as a hunter. There were two other Lewis and Clark men among the forty-two trappers and *voyageurs* on the boat, John Potts and Peter Wiser. None of the three had long to live.

It was fitting that Manuel Lisa should be the first of the St. Louis traders to start with a company for the upper Missouri. Not only was he a veteran in Indian country, but he was bolder, more intelligent, more perspicacious and more vigorous than most of the others. He was also, in numerous ways, unscrupulous, but he had no advantage in this respect.

Lisa had established himself in St. Louis in 1790, but before that year he was widely known in lower Louisiana for his daring and competence. The Spanish gov-

---

[17] Spelled "Drewyer" by them.

ernment had given him the exclusive right to trade with the Osages, not only a valuable grant but one which indicated his reputation and position, for the same privilege had been held for twenty years by the distinguished Choteau family. A man of many contrasts, Lisa was given to intermittent dark moods, outbursts of wild vigor, gay song, fury and kindness, which made him an enigma to other traders and to those who worked for him. Had he lived in the days of the Spanish conquests he undoubtedly would have ranked as one of the greatest *conquistadores*.

The expedition advanced without serious trouble to the mouth of the Osage River.[18] There one of the *engages,* Antoine Bissonette, deserted. Infuriated by the disloyal act, Lisa sent Drouillard to bring him back dead or alive. Drouillard, the disciplined soldier, overtook Bissonette, and in a struggle wounded him. Lisa's attitude immediately became one of mercy. He put the wounded deserter in a canoe with two paddlers and sent him back to St. Louis. Bissonette died en route.

Shortly after the company had passed the Platte, the suspicious eyes of a lookout traversing the river and the distant bluffs were held by a small dark object on the water ahead. In the dancing sun waves it appeared like a black stick. The lookout cupped his hands over his face. *"Il est extraordinaire,"* he muttered. "It moves like a canoe." The words brought heads around.

It was a canoe. John Colter was coming down the Missouri alone. With mingled joy and astonishment, the men of the keelboat watched him approach, a gaunt figure in smoke-blackened buckskin who had performed

---

[18] Near the present Jefferson City, Missouri.

the amazing feat of slipping through all the northern Indian Country, passed the Mandans, the Aricaras, the Sioux, in his frail little craft. Drouillard, Wiser and Potts gave their old companion a noisy welcome.

As for Lisa, if he had never known Colter, there was no man he would have preferred to meet at the time. Colter had been where he was going. As an adviser and guide, Colter would be invaluable. Lisa quickly set about inducing him to turn back with the company.

After leaving Lewis and Clark, Colter had trapped with Dickson and Hancock for a time on the Yellowstone, but he had found his companions less agreeable than he had expected them to be, and he had lost interest in the venture. With the first signs of spring he had set out alone for St. Louis.

Colter had not seen a white woman, had not slept in a feather bed, had not put his feet under a cloth-covered table, for more than three years. He had known only the hardships, the constant dangers and privations, the heavy stillness of an unbounded wilderness. Yet, his craving for the amenities of civilization was not strong enough for him to reject Lisa's offer. He agreed to turn back once more.

It was a decision which would shed new light where only darkness prevailed in the mountain west, give the nation new knowledge of western geography, open unknown trails, and produce one of the most stirring and dramatic stories of exploration and discovery in all history.

By a show of fearlessness and force, by firing warning bursts from the two swivel guns mounted on the bow of his keelboat, Lisa pushed through the Sioux, the treacherous Aricaras, the threatening Assiniboines, and turned up the Yellowstone to the mouth of its principal tributary, the Big Horn. There on the right bank of the confluence he erected the first American trading post on the upper Missouri River system.

The choice of the location was a grave mistake.

The expedition with which Gros Blanc was to travel was not ready to leave St. Louis until late in May, more than a month after Lisa had departed. In it, in addition to the chief's party, were two small military escorts, and two trading groups. Lieutenant Joseph Kimball would turn back after seeing that the Sioux deputation, which consisted of eighteen men, women and children, had reached its homeland. Ensign Nathaniel Pryor and the handful of enlisted men under his command would deliver Gros Blanc to the Mandans.

The small trading companies were led by Auguste Pierre Chouteau, a graduate of West Point, and Pierre Dorion, Junior, son of the famous Lewis and Clark interpreter. Chouteau, with thirty-two men, was going to trade with the Mandans. The destination of young Dorion and his ten *voyageurs* was the country of the Yankton Sioux. There were nearly a hundred persons in the joint expedition.

The boats made slow headway, but passage through the lower river tribes and the Sioux was accomplished without a major difficulty. Lieutenant Kimball turned back after completing his assignment. Dorion departed on his scheduled mission. Ensign Pryor and Chouteau reached the Arikara Villages on September 9. They were greeted with bursts of gunfire.

The Arikaras were at war with the Mandans. They had been informed by Lisa that soldiers were escorting the chief, Gros Blanc, to the Mandan Villages, and they had determined not to let him pass. Yet, this was not the only reason for their violent actions against Pryor and Chouteau. In the parleys which ensued, interpreters picked up the intelligence that British agents recently had been among the tribes of the upper river urging them to attack American trading companies. The agents had been lavish with gifts, and they had alarmed numerous chiefs with stories that the Americans intended to drive all Indians from their ancestral homes and take their hunting grounds from them. If the British were obliged to recognize the legality of the transaction which had brought Louisiana Territory under the American flag, they had no intention of abandoning the lucrative fur trade which they had enjoyed for so many years among the Indians living near the international border. They would do all they could to prevent the St. Louis traders from establishing themselves in that immense area, which ran from Lake Superior to the mountains, even to the extent of starting uprisings and tribal wars.

All efforts of Pryor and Chouteau to achieve a peaceful solution of the situation failed. The Arikaras closed their ears. They would not even trade with Chouteau. Suddenly they began an attack on the boats.

The fight was short but vicious. Greatly outnumbered, the Americans were forced to retreat. Four of them were killed, nine were grievously wounded. Pryor wanted to make an attempt to get around the Arikaras by land, but neither Gros Blanc nor others with long experience in the Indian Country thought the proposal feasible. The expedition turned back to St. Louis.

Gros Blanc would be obliged to wait for more than two years before the government and the United States army found a way to get him safety back to his people. The man who would accomplish the feat was Manuel Lisa.[19]

Long before he had reached the confluence of the Missouri and Yellowstone Rivers, the Blackfeet knew Lisa was coming. Such intelligence traveled swiftly through the Indian country. Lisa had announced that his chief purpose was to open trade with the Blackfeet as well as other Indians above the Mandans. Doubtless John Colter persuaded him to change his plans.

Colter knew the Blackfeet for what they were: proud,

---

[19] These two expeditions are the only ones shown by historical records to have gone out to the northern river country in 1807. Yet, there must have been another.

While at his post on Lake Invermere in British Columbia, the famed Canadian explorer, David Thompson, received two letters by Indian bearers. The first, dated July 1807, had been sent from a place called Fort Lewis, Yellow River, Columbia. The second letter, bearing the date September 29, 1807, came from Poltito Palton Lake, also allegedly in the Columbia Valley. Both purportedly were signed by American army officers, the first by a Captain Perch and a Lieutenant Roseman, the second by a Lieutenant Jeremy Pinch. Pinch's letter upbraided Thompson for not acknowledging receipt of the first message, which informed him of American trading regulations, and threatened the use of force to halt British traders from selling arms to hostile Indians in American territory. Pinch assertedly had forty-two men under him.

Thompson's own journal in August 1807, notes the arrival of Pinch "at the confluence of the two most southern and considerable branches of the Columbia." Who authorized the American military expedition, or how it got to the Columbia Valley — if, indeed, there was such an expedition — has not been determined. Perch, Roseman and Pinch do not appear in records of the time, nor do the names of the places mentioned in their letters. Yet, someone was there, and someone wrote the letters and sent them to Thompson by Indian messengers. The suggestion has been made that the men were American trappers, not soldiers, who were attempting to keep the British out of the Columbia, an area rich in furs, but there is no evidence to support such a conclusion.

jealous of their hunting grounds, unfriendly and dangerous. If they tolerated a few British traders, it did not
mean they would react in the same manner to Americans.
Captain Lewis had had trouble with them, had mortally
wounded one with his rifle while another was fatally
stabbed by R. Fields, a soldier, in an unavoidable fight.
Colter had been up and down the Yellowstone, with both
the Lewis and Clark Expedition and the trappers, Dickson and Hancock. He knew it abounded in furs. Lisa,
he contended, would do better, be safer and have an
easier journey by going up it.

Lisa followed Colter's advice, and in so doing created
a gulf between American traders and the Blackfeet that
would remain unbridged for three decades. As they observed Lisa's company, the Blackfeet could draw only
one conclusion. The Yellowstone and the Big Horn
flowed through the heart of Absaroka, the homeland of
the Crows, their oldest and worst enemies. Obviously
Americans not only preferred to trade with the Crows
but were in league with them.

Relentless war against the new intruders was the only
course the Blackfeet saw open. It was begun. The toll
of trappers would be heavy before it ended.

The building of Fort Lisa on the Big Horn had no
more than begun before Lisa asked Colter to go among
the surrounding tribes and announce the establishment
of the post. Colter was given no specific route to follow,
for it was not known where the villages would be found.
Lisa did express the belief he should go south and southwest, along the eastern front of the ranges, and possibly
he suggested that Colter should visit the Three Forks.
It seems doubtful that he would advocate crossing the

mountains in the face of approaching winter. Moreover, it would have been illogical to assume that Indians would travel from the western slope to the Big Horn to trade. If the great distance did not make such a journey infeasible, the difficulties and dangers to be met would dissuade them from making the attempt.

The aspens had turned to gold when Colter left Fort Lisa. He went on foot, on his back a thirty pound back containing food staples and extra clothing, a supply of ammunition in a leather pouch at his belt, a rifle in the crook of his arm.

There is nothing in the accounts of the period, written by men who knew him, to indicate that he hesitated to go alone on such a perilous journey into an unknown country at the late season of the year. There is, in fact, no record to suggest that he did not look forward to going. Rather, what he did suggests the opposite attitude.

The route Colter took has been fairly well established, but which way he traveled over it has never been determined. Obviously his direction was known to those to whom he reported, but they neglected to note it in their own recounting. It hardly matters.

If one accepts the belief that Colter traveled as the clock hands, he went up the Big Horn. Somewhere in the upper valley – probably on Wind River – he met the Crows in their winter encampment. After informing them that their trade would be most welcome at the post, he announced his wish to proceed westward through some of the most rugged country and highest mountains on the continent. A party – the exact number is not known, but probably was no more than ten or twelve – agreed to guide him. They traveled on horses.

The gigantic Wind River Range was crossed through Two-gwo-tee Pass. Before him was Jackson's Hole, the lovely lakes and the Snake River, and beyond them the majestic wall of the Tetons.

An American Mountain Man had crossed the Continental Divide to Pacific waters, traveling through country unknown to the civilized world.

Colter must have been looking for something. He had now gone beyond the possible trading area of the post far behind him on the Big Horn. The best guess seems to be that he was looking for a river which he believed existed and which would lead him to the Spanish settlements of the Southwest. The Indians would have told him that no such river was to be found in Jackson's Hole, that the Snake went westward and northwestward and eventually emptied into a great river that reached the western sea. Colter knew that river – the Columbia – he had spent a year on it. If the Indians told him about the Green, which rose to the south, and flowed in the direction of the Spanish settlements, he must have decided that it was too far away to be reached on his present trip, or that it was not the river he sought.

With his guides he went across the Snake, through the deep snow drifts of Teton Pass – it was January, 1808 – and reached Pierre's Hole, the beautiful valley west of the Tetons. On the westward side of the pass, Colter picked up a rounded rock. By chipping he gave it the resemblance of a human head. On it he cut his name and the figures 1808.[20]

In Pierre's Hole, Colter and the Crows were attacked

[20] The rock was found in 1931. It was given to the museum in Grand Teton National Park.

by a band of Blackfeet. Colter received a severe leg wound. The Blackfeet were sent fleeing in retreat.

The encounter, isolated and brief, was to become highly significant. If there had been any doubt in the minds of the Blackfeet that the white traders were in league with their deadliest enemies, there was none now. A Mountain Man had been seen fighting against them, displaying great bravery, with the Crows.

Following the battle, Colter's guides left him, fearing reprisals from a larger number of Blackfeet. Alone once more, after recrossing Teton Pass to Jackson's Hole, he set out to find the most direct route back to Fort Lisa. His sense of direction and his knowledge of topography were nothing less than phenomenal. He turned up the Lewis River, passed Lewis Lake and came to a much larger lake – the Yellowstone. About it great geysers shot columns of water into the wintry air, hot springs bubbled and colored fountains boiled over wierd terraces.

He had discovered the wonderland that was to become Yellowstone National Park. Later, when he had returned to St. Louis and would speak of the amazing things he had seen there, such as hot mud pots and cauldrons steaming in snowbanks, his listeners would smile knowingly and touch their heads. Colter had been too long alone in the wilderness.

Going on he broke a trail from the southwest to the northeast, reaching the North Fork of the Stinking Water River.[21] It led him northeast, winding in its canyons through the great peaks of the Absaroka Range to the Big Horn River and his outbound trail.

---

[21] Which some chamber of commerce persons, affecting sensitivity, managed to change to Shoshone.

It was spring when Colter reached Fort Lisa.[22] Other
Mountain Men had been sent out. Edward Rose had
gone among the Crows with several packhorses carrying
merchandise, but had proved to be a poor trader — or a
dishonest one — and had returned with little to show for
his trip. After a fight with an unfuriated Lisa, Rose had
ridden away to live as an Indian. George Drouillard and
three other trappers had gone southwestward into the
Bighorn Basin. Drouillard had stayed there, but his companions had gone on, crossing the Continental Divide
and had been the first Mountain Men to reach Green
River, which would be the scene of so many important
events in the fur trade in years to come.

As spring advanced, Lisa put two plans into operation.
He dispatched men to trap the streams which joined
at the Three Forks to form the Missouri — the Gallatin,
Jefferson and Madison — and he sent Colter as a peace
emissary to the Blackfeet. Probably no more difficult or
perilous journey was ever assigned to a Mountain Man.

Without requesting time to rest from his great winter
journey of six or seven hundred miles, Colter started with
the band going to the Three Forks, but left them after a
journey of little more than a hundred miles, and struck
out alone. Instead of finding Blackfeet, he fell in with
eight hundred Crows and Flatheads on the Gallatin River.

The Blackfeet were not far away, however, and some
fifteen hundred of them suddenly attacked. Once more
Colter had no alternative, if he would save his own life,
but to fight with the Crows.

A terrible slaughter took place. Although greatly outnumbered, the Crows and Flatheads, with the help of

---

[22] Also called Fort Manuel, and Fort Raymond, after Lisa's son.

Colter's deadly gun, were victorious. The Blackfeet were driven from a field that was strewn with corpses.

There was no hope now that a reconciliation with the Blackfeet could be achieved, and Colter abandoned the idea and rejoined the trappers at the Three Forks. It was fall and the cottonwoods and aspens of the high country were turning. With John Potts, his companion of the Lewis and Clark Expedition, Colter trapped on the Jefferson, using a small canoe. Exercising extreme caution, they concealed themselves during the day and visited their traps only at dawn and dusk.

Early one morning they were descending a small tributary of the Jefferson when they were suddenly confronted by an immense band of Blackfeet, numbering between five and six hundred warriors.

One man would give to the world the only authentic account of the terrible and miraculous events which took place on the unnamed creek that fall day in 1808. John Bradbury, the British naturalist and explorer would write in his *Travels In America* what he heard from Colter's lips when he talked with the famed Mountain Men at St. Louis in the spring of 1810.

Retreat for Colter and Potts was impossible, and Colter saw wisdom in obeying the Indians' command to land. He stepped out of the canoe, making signs of friendship, clinging to the hope that he could convince the Blackfeet of his good intentions, but Potts refused to obey and made a sudden attempt to push off in the canoe. An arrow struck him. He fired and killed a brave. A shower of arrows and lances tore through his body and it toppled into the water, a riddled bloody mass.

Colter was stripped naked, and the Indians began a council to determine how he would be put to death. Now, in the words of John Bradbury:[23]

They were first inclined to set him up as a mark to shoot at; but the chief interfered, and seizing him by the shoulder, asked if he could run fast . . . He knew that he had now to run for his life, with the dreadful odds of five or six hundred against him, and those armed Indians; therefore he cunningly replied that he was a very bad runner . . . The chief now commanded the party to remain stationary, and let Colter out on the prairie three or four hundred yards, and released him, bidding him *to save himself if he could*. . . Colter . . . ran with a speed at which he himself was surprised.

Colter ran three miles before he looked back. He had left far behind all but one Indian, who carried a spear.

A faint gleam of hope now cheered the heart of Colter . . . but that confidence was nearly fatal to him, for he exerted himself to such a degree, that blood gushed from nostrils . . . He had now arrived within a mile of the river, when he distinctly heard the appalling sound of foot-steps behind him. . . Again he turned his head and saw the savage not twenty yards from him. . . he suddenly stopped, turned around, and spread out his arms. The Indian, sur-prised by the suddenness of the action, and perhaps of the bloody appearance of Colter, also attempted to stop; but exhausted with running, he fell whilst endeavoring to throw his spear, which stuck in the ground and broke in his hand. Colter instantly snatched up the pointed part . . .

Leaving the Indian dying with the broken spear em-

---

[23] See Stallo Vinton, *John Colter,* New York, 1926; John Bradbury, *op. cit.*; Burton Harris, *John Colter: his years in the Rockies,* New York, 1952.

bedded in his chest, Colter ran on. He was struggling with the last vestige of his strength to keep himself from fainting when he reached the Jefferson and plunged into the cold water.

> Fortunately for him, a little below this place there was an island, against the upper part of which a raft of drift timber had lodged. He dived under the raft, and after several efforts, got his head above water amongst the trunk of trees, covered over with smaller wood to the depth of several feet.

A large number of Indians were soon on the scene, howling and yelping in their dismay and anger. Dusk was falling before they gave up hope of finding their quarry and left. Colter then

> swam silently down the river to a considerable distance, when he landed and travelled all night. Although happy in having escaped from the Indians, his situation was still dreadful: he was completely naked, under a burning sun; the sole of his feet were entirely filled with thorns of the prickly pear; he was hungry, and he had no means of killing game . . . and was at least seven days' journey from Lisa's fort, on the Big Horn branch of the Roche Jaune River. These were circumstances under which almost any man but an American hunter would have despaired.

Hardly a questionable assertion.

Colter survived on roots and berries. Seven days later the lookout at Fort Lisa saw approaching a form which appeared to be anything but human. It was naked, bloody, filthy, covered with welts and scars and torn flesh. It weaved as it came toward the post gate. Colter fell into the arms of the men who ran out to him.

In a comparative sense, St. Louis traders talked *big business* during the winter of 1808-1809. Projected proposals and plans involved larger expeditions and greater expenditures than had ever been conceived in previous years. But never before had prospects looked so good. Never before had they known such great opportunities.

Lisa and Drouillard with a crew of *voyageurs* had come down the river from the Big Horn in the early fall of 1808. Drouillard was promptly charged with the murder of the *engage,* Antoine Bissonette, and brought to trial. It would have been difficult to find men in St. Louis who would display sympathy for a deserter. The success or failure of a company in the wilderness might well depend upon the loyalty and obedience of a single employee. The maintenance of discipline was essential, and a leader had every right to enforce it. If the law did not condone violent punitive measures, public opinions did. A jury quickly acquited Drouillard.

Lisa's operations had confirmed Lewis and Clark's reports. The far upper rivers and the northern mountains were unbelievably rich in furs. He had not brought a great many back with him, but that circumstance was attributed to the difficulties of opening the country, of learning its geography, and of establishing trade with the Indians. All these things took time. Yet, he had brought back more than two tons of pelts of various kinds, most important among them two thousand or more prime beaver skins in thirty packs. His return would be in excess of $10,000. Moreover, his operation on the Big Horn was continuing. There was every reason to be encouraged. He had left hunting plans for the fall, winter and spring. (Lisa's orders would be carried out by the men on the Big Horn during his absence. Again they would defy the Blackfeet at the Three Forks. Again they would travel far south and southwest to the Wind River, across the divide to the Green, into great mountain valleys and along streams never before seen by white men.)

Optimism, enthusiasm and dreams colored practicality and overshadowed the lessons of experience. Lisa was the guiding spirit, and action revolved around him. The new association that was formed was called the St. Louis Missouri Fur Company, but the St. Louis would soon disappear from its name in popular usage. The firm of Lisa, Menard & Morrison was absorbed, its assets purchased.

Virtually all the prominent businessmen in the city, subscribing more than $40,000 to the treasury, signed the articles of incorporation that gave the new company legality and life. Benjamin Wilkinson, Pierre Chouteau, Sr., Manuel Lisa, Auguste Chouteau, Jr., Reuben Lewis, William Clark, Sylvester Labadie, Pierre Menard, William Morrison, Andrew Henry, Dennis Fitz Hugh signed in that order. Lisa and Wilkinson were named chief factors and would transact business with the Indians. General Clark would be in command in St. Louis. The others would be assigned various missions and duties from time to time.

If they did not know the word *logistics,* they knew its meaning, and they knew the ordeals to be faced in wilderness transport and supply. These were formidable. Hardly less complicated and difficult were the problems of Indian Country merchandising, such things as selection, quality, quantity and presentation.

British manufactured goods were greatly superior to those made in America. This was not a discovery of St. Louis suppliers and merchants. The Indians had come to understand it soon after the first American fur traders pushed over the eastern mountains with articles produced in the cities of the Atlantic coast. American products were poorly made. American blankets and cloth were shoddy. American cooking pots and other utensils contained inferior materials. American gunpowder was generally second quality. American whiskey was not only raw but was highly diluted, and sometimes poisonous. American traps and axe heads and knives and other tools were brittle. The colors and gilt of American ornaments faded. Yet, the prices charged by American traders were always as high, and usually higher, than prices charged by the Canadians for better goods. American scales could be depended upon to register dishonest weight, always in favor of their owners, of course.

Whatever else they might be — savage, cruel, filthy — Indians, and especially those of the northern forests and plains, were not stupid. A craving to possess the weapons and manufactured products of the white man — all of them luxuries — might temporarily decrease their sales resistance, and liquor was certain to do that, but these were forces which created conditions that could not be depended upon to endure.

The men who organized the Missouri Fur Company in 1809 had no illusions in this respect. To meet Canadian competition, they had to offer British goods, and they had to undersell the Canadians.

A tin tea kettle, then, had to be purchased in England, shipped to New Orleans, brought up the Mississippi by keelboat to St. Louis. There it had to be placed in a pack on another keelboat and taken by more brute strength to the upper Missouri, perhaps up the Yellowstone and the Big Horn. It might have to be carried far beyond those points, hundreds of miles by pack-animal, into the mountains, before it passed across a trading robe in exchange for beaver pelts.

It is approximately eight thousand miles from Liverpool to the confluence of the Yellowstone and Big Horn rivers. Orders for goods might reach England from St. Louis – going overland by express to New York and then by fast mail ship across the North Atlantic – in nine or ten weeks. It could, and often did, due to blizzards and gales, take twice as long. Shipments of British goods, even though they moved directly to New Orleans, took from six to eight months to reach St. Louis.

Buying from the manufacturers in England was the cheapest way to obtain trade goods, in spite of the great distance they must travel. Also, it was the slowest way. To be safe, a St. Louis trader had to order goods a year before he would need them.

The fastest method was to buy the goods in New York or Philadelphia, but this added a middleman's or wholesaler's profit to the cost, and it often was high. The eastern supplier had to pay the cost of transporting the merchandise across the sea, and he included this cost in his price as well as a profit for himself. From New York or Philadelphia the goods might be sent overland to the Ohio, thence travel by that river and the Mississippi to St. Louis, or they might be sent by ship to New Orleans.

John Jacob Astor was still a young man when he

realized that a large amount of money was to be made in supplying traders, even his competitors, with British goods. Before the purchase of Louisiana, he enjoyed a large business with traders in the Old Northwest, and even sold goods to French companies operating west of the Great Lakes and the Mississippi out of St. Louis and New Orleans. After the trans-Mississippi region came under the American flag, he quickly became the largest wholesaler for the fur trade in New York.

Possessing enormous purchasing power, and owning cargo vessels, Astor could buy more cheaply in England than smaller companies and transport goods more cheaply to New York. In his New York emporium a western trader could obtain everything from a package of needles to a swivel gun, a good British blanket or a string of glass beads, a tin teakettle or a keg of gunpowder. Astor would gladly supply a trader whose business he was planning to steal as quickly as he would sell to one with whom he was already in deadly competition. Astor understood that price, distribution, availability and quality, composed the foundation of successful merchandising, and he was in a better positon than anyone else to provide them. He permitted a rival to survive only until he chose to smash him, and few traders survived after Astor had set out to destroy them.

In the year 1809, however, Astor had not yet chosen to move the incomparable forces of his American Fur Company into the Missouri River trade. He would get around to that, but not before he thought the time propitious. Meanwhile, he would be glad to send a tin teakettle out to St. Louis.

Suppose it cost him twenty cents in England. Transportation, insurance, handling, import tax, license, etc., would add another twenty cents. Total: 40 cents. To this he would add a markup of 200 per cent, or 80 cents. (Not unusual on goods sold to traders.) Total: $1.20.

If the Missouri Fur Company was the buyer, it would add to the purchase price of $1.20, about 50 per cent, or 60 cents, for wages, transportation up the Missouri, etc. Total: $1.80. To this the MFC would add a mark-up of 200 per cent, or $3.60. Total: $5.40.

The Indian purchaser would not pay the $5.40 with coin. He would pay with beaver skins, possibly four prime pelts weighing six or seven pounds.

The MFC would charge off 25 cents for transporting the four skins down the river to St. Louis. They would bring $4.00 a pound from Astor. Total: $28.00. Less 25 cents freight cost, $27.75.

Allowing for normal losses and all other expenses, the MFC made more than $25.00 profit on the teakettle-four-pelt deal.

Cost to Astor of the four skins (purchase price, plus shipping to London) was $30.00. Astor would sell the skins in London for $8.00 a pound, or $56.00. Profit to Astor on the skins alone would be $26.00.

With profits varying between 200 and 700 per cent, suppliers, traders and fur merchants were in a good position to grow rich in a short time. The theory was good, but the reality often brought contrary results.

It took far more time to load a keelboat and start it up the river than it did for the river to destroy it. A single snag, a drifting timber, a hidden rock could do that so swiftly that the men aboard on such an occasion often did not have time to save themselves. The bodies of *voyageurs* and hunters not infrequently washed down the mad current with the profits of an entire season.

But they were not men whose lives were influenced and directed by economic considerations more than by other forces. Of all the pursuits, of all the callings in which Americans engaged in the first years of the nineteenth century, this was truer of the Mountain Men than of any others. They went out to find, to see, to discover, to unveil, to adventure—not only to sell tin teakettles to Indians.

The big 1809 expedition of the Missouri Fur Company left St. Louis in early June, and with its departure began the first attempt to secure a monopoly on the fur trade of the upper rivers.

The Federal government was still suffering from the nasty headache which developed from its efforts to get its guest, Chief Gros Blanc of the Mandans, safely back to his people. Now Governor Meriwether Lewis saw an opportunity to accomplish the task and save face for the president. The expedition of the MFC consisted of two hundred men, all well-armed, and nine boats carrying swivel guns. The army could not produce a more formidable force on the Missouri, and Lewis preferred to entrust the life of Gros Blanc to Mountain Men than to soldiers who had little or no knowledge of Indians or the ways of the wilderness.

Governor Lewis contracted with the MFC to escort Blanc to the Mandans. Under the terms of the agreement, suitable quarters for a distinguished chief, his family and retinue, were to be provided on one of the boats. They were to be fully guarded at all times by at least fifty marksmen. For this service, the MFC would receive $3,000 when the journey started, and another $3,000 when the governor was officially informed that Gros Blanc had been delivered whole to his home.

It was very good business for the MFC. The money would go far toward paying the expenses of the company for the season. But the shrewd partners weren't satisfied. They took advantage of Lewis's anxiety to further improve their own prospects. They exacted from Lewis a promise that he would not license any other traders to ascend above the mouth of the Platte until they had been given time to get far beyond it. Other trading parties, they maintained, might jeopardize their relations with the Indians. Lewis saw through the demand, but he was not in a position to reject it. However, he had another card of his own to play.

The last military establishment which the expedition would pass was Fort Osage.[24] It housed a small garrison commanded by Captain Eli B. Clemson, and a government trading post (called a factory), the only one ever built west of the Mississippi. Captain Clemson, obeying orders forwarded by Governor Lewis, swore in the entire MFC as militia. This had the effect of placing the expedition under federal jurisdiction until its official mission had been completed. Pierre Chouteau was placed in command.

The MFC partners, all but one of whom were aboard the boats, were no more delighted by the outlook than was the St. Louis *Louisiana Gazette,* which had predicted on March 8th that the company had "every prospect of becoming a source of incalculable advantage not only

---

[24] Near the present Sibley, Missouri, east of Kansas City.

to the individuals engaged but to the community at large. Their extensive preparations, and the extensive force with which they intend to ascend the Missouri, may bid defiance to any hostile force they may meet with. The streams which descend from the Rocky Mountains afford the finest of hunting, and here, we learn, they intend to build their fort."

Neither the Sioux nor the Arikaras had the stomach to attack the expedition. Menacing gestures and shouted threats marked the extent of their opposition. The Mandans were reached on September 24th, and Gros Blanc was joyously received by his people, who had begun to believe they would never see him again.

Wasting no time, the company pressed on. At the mouth of the Big Knife River, a party was left to erect a post, called Fort Mandan. Here several of the partners, including Lisa and Pierre Chouteau, started back to St. Louis.

Fort Lisa on the Big Horn was reached near the end of October. It was too late in the year to carry out the plan to build a post at the Three Forks, but groups were dispatched to the Crow Country as soon as horses were obtained from the Indians. Not many weeks had passed before packs of furs were brought into the post, and throughout most of the winter they continued to arrive, were processed, graded and baled for shipment down the river.

It was in March 1810, that Pierre Menard and Andrew Henry, *bourgeois* and field captain respectively, with Colter serving as guide, started with a company of forty or forty-five hunters, among them several French Canadians and Delaware Indians, on the trail to the Three

Forks. All were mounted, and they had pack animals to carry their traps, trade goods and supplies.

No intelligence regarding the temper of the Blackfeet had been received during the winter. It was still hoped that new opportunities to establish amicable relations with them might appear. Meanwhile, a fort would be built from which intensive trapping operations would be conducted.

No Indians were encountered on the way. The site selected for the fort was on a neck of land between the Jefferson and Madison rivers, about two miles above their confluence, and not far from the scene of Colter's miraculous escape. With a stockade erected into which they could retreat and which would afford protection for their horses, the trappers began to work the surrounding territory. They found an incredible number of beaver. So large was their daily catch that it was believed they would take out at least three hundred packs during the season. This was in itself a veritable fortune, amounting to no less than $120,000. When added to the large number of packs of various furs already at Fort Lisa, and others which would be brought in during the summer, the returns of the company's first year would be beyond the most optimistic expectations.

Then out of the dense forest on the morning of April 12th, the Blackfeet struck. Most of the trappers succeeded in fighting their way back to the stockade, but five of them died, and their furs and traps were captured.

The Blackfeet vanished as silently as they had come. The hunters went back to work, but they kept close together, sent out scouts and held a certain number in reserve at the fort. The Blackfeet had not left the area.

This was established by signs the men discovered. Trapping was carried on with difficulty, and always in the constant fear that another attack would come.

It came. Drouillard and two others were killed.

Further operations, it appeared, would be unrewarding, and could be carried on only at the risk of a great loss of life. Menard proposed abandoning the hunt altogether, but Henry refused. At last it was decided that Menard, with ten or twelve men who also wanted to leave, would take the furs already collected back to Fort Lisa. Colter again would be their guide.[25]

Andrew Henry's obduracy and courage underwrote his fame as a Mountain Man. For three months more he and his intrepid men defied the Blackfeet and attempted to take beaver. They were almost constantly harassed. That any of them survived was the result of their strategy. They scouted a stream carefully before setting traps on it. They maintained a constant vigil, then scouted the stream again before taking the beaver which had been trapped.

In sporadic attacks several of them were killed. In one major fight, twenty trappers stood off more than two hundred Blackfeet, lost only one of their number, and killed twenty or thirty Indians.

At last, even the redoubtable Henry was obliged to admit the futility of attempting to continue. But instead of retreating to Fort Lisa, he turned south into the mountains. The first snows of winter already had fallen on the great peaks when he led his little mounted band up the Madison Valley. The Continental Divide was

---

[25]After reaching Fort Lisa, Menard went at once down the river to St. Louis.

crossed (probably through Targhee Pass) just west of
the fabulous land of geysers Colter had found. This was
country white men had never entered. Descending the
western slope, they found a lake out of which a large
stream flowed. It was a branch of the Snake. Both the
lake and the stream were given Henry's name.

Following down Henry's Fork, through deep canyons
and past roaring falls and cataracts, they stopped at last
and built a small fort.[26] It was the first American trading post erected west of the Rocky Mountains. The
waters passing its stockade were a part of the enormous
Columbia River system, and reached the Pacific.

No Indians came to trouble them, but to their great
disappointment they found very little game in the country. They had taken a number of beaver on their journey
through the mountains, and they took more in the creeks
which tumbled from the high forests into Henry's Fork,
but a beaver, except a part of its tail, was poor food.
Winter arrived in a series of blizzards, and the men were
locked in their small cabins. The last beaver tail was
devoured. The last of their staples was consumed. Now
and then, by persistent hunting in the deep snow through
the barren land they luckily killed a few rabbits, and
occasionally a deer or an elk. It was not enough. One
by one through the dreadful winter they ate their horses.

When the first warming days of the spring had come,
Henry could no longer hold his men together. He gave
them their discharges. Several of them, perhaps dreaming of a warm climate, set out for the Spanish settlements.
In time, vague reports gave rise to the belief that they
reached them, or at least some of them did. No one
could be sure.

---

[26] Near the present St. Anthony, Idaho.

The mind of one man had broken, and he wandered off into the unknown alone, never to be heard of again.

Several others struck out eastward. It was confirmed that at least three of this group were on the lower Missouri River in May. They had not passed through Fort Lisa en route, so must have traveled in a more direct course through the mountains and across the plains. The fate of their companions remained a mystery.

How many men elected to stay with Henry was a fact the early historians – if they ever knew – neglected to record. The number could hardly have been more than three or four, but, however many companions he had, he and they performed an amazing feat of exploration. Somehow they obtained more horses – perhaps from Snakes or Flatheads – and ascending the Snake they came to a pass through a great range to the east. It was probably the Hoback River. In time they reached the upper Green River.

If Henry and his men did not know where they were, and if they had no geographical names to note in their accounts, it would have been difficult for them to state with any accuracy where they had been. The best they could do was to describe the ranges and rivers they saw and passed.

That was enough, however, to make it fairly certain that they went down the Green a considerable distance. Turning up some tributary, possibly the Sandy or one of its branches, they worked their way by some unidentified trails to the Big Horn. They had come very close to discovering the famous South Pass.[27]

In July 1810, they reached Fort Mandan. Sad news awaited them. A post the company had built at Cedar

---

[27] Some historians insist that they did traverse the South Pass.

Island for the Sioux trade had burned. Furs valued at $15,000 had been destroyed by the fire. The post on the Big Horn had been abandoned. All efforts to trade above the Mandans had been discontinued. The price of furs in New York had fallen from $4.00 to $2.50 a pound, and there were few buyers.

The original capital, $40,000, had been saved, but otherwise there was little to show for the year's work. Most of the partners wanted their investment, and arrangements would be made to sell all remaining assets.

The first Missouri Fur Company had failed.

The Mountain Men had gone out. The story they wrote in the first seven years after the Louisiana Purchase was more than impressive, it was an unparalleled record of exploration and discovery.

There had not been many of them in those first years. There never would be many of them. From the day the Lewis and Clark Expedition saw a canoe on the shore to the breaking of the trails across the deserts to California, in the late 1820s, there would be no more than three hundred.

These three hundred were the men who participated in original discoveries, and most of them were followers rather than leaders. Yet, all of them went out there into the unknown, and if they did not command, they fought to break through, they won and deserved the title of Mountain Man. It was more than a title designating achievement in penetrating one of the largest wilderness areas on earth. It was a title of honor, signifying rare courage and intrepedity.

The War of 1812 would hamper them. Commerce

was interrupted, even halted at times, between the frontier and the eastern seaboard. Trade goods were difficult,
if not impossible, to obtain, for the Atlantic was block-
aded by the British. Getting furs from the West to New
York was a precarious undertaking which usually resulted
in heavy losses to those who attempted it. Those, that
is, except Astor. Political influence, bribes to government officials, and smuggling helped him to grow richer
while all other traders grew poorer or went broke.

The overland Astorians, however, would be on their
way when the war clouds gathered, and they would break
new trails that would wreathe their names in glory.

The many paths of Hoback, Miller, Robinson, Rezner,
Cass, Carson, Delauney, St. Michael, Dubreuil, La Cha-
pelle, Turcot and Landry would never be marked accur-
ately on maps, but they opened vast unknown territories.
Some of them would come upon a river, and they would
grow excited, for they thought it flowed into the Pacific
Ocean. They would follow it for a time, and they would
see ahead of them a white desert reaching into the western sky and in it the river vanished. The water they
would see under the haze of distance would not be that
of the Pacific.

They would be the first to gaze into the valley of the
Great Salt Lake.

Robert Stuart and his six companions, returning east
to report the tragic events at Astoria, would open a way
that would become the great western artery of the nation's
economy. They would break a trail down the Platte to
the Missouri – the route of the Oregon Trail across the
plains.

Jedediah Smith, Sylvester Pattie and Ewing Young

would take their bands to Spanish California, and some
of them would circle back, finding more deserts and more
mountains which had never known the tread of white
man's moccasin.

In less than three decades after it had become part
of the United States, the Far West would be opened by
the Mountain Men. Within that short span of years they
would know every major geographical feature in it, and
their graves would mark the ways they had gone.

1810

TURNING NUMBER TWO

———◆———

The Wide Horizon

Private capital for the first time
attempts to expand the American
economic empire to the Columbia
Basin and North Pacific Coast

II

The Wide Horizon

If Astor's plan was diabolical in its aspects,
so was it admirable. If it was piratical,
so was it commendable, so did it enhance
the national interest. If it was selfish,
so was it more vital, more dynamic,
more momentous, than any plan ever
originated and carried forward by
one man in the history of America.

from *Furs by Astor*

John Jacob Astor had not only held the same thoughts about the West as Thomas Jefferson, but he had held them first. Moreover, he had acted on them to an extent Jefferson would like to have done but was unable to accomplish because of political opposition.

The enormity and boldness of Astor's plan delineated the measure of the man who had conceived it. He was setting out to do what nations, with all their civil, military and financial resources, hesitated to attempt. He was casting himself in the role of supreme ruler of an earthly domain into which all the countries of Europe could have been dropped and lost from sight. He was appropriating for himself the prerogatives of an economic royalist and the rights and privileges of an indisputable sovereign.[1]

---

[1] See Chittenden, *History of American Fur Trade;* Kenneth W. Porter, *John Jacob Astor, Business Man,* Cambridge, 1931; Terrell, *Furs by Astor;*

Astor had long maintained that the United States could never know any security as long as it was flanked on three sides by foreign powers. He had looked on France as a greater menace than England and Spain together. This often-expressed opinion, however, unquestionably had been influenced by both his profound hatred of Napoleon and his faith in the integrity of England's government, despite the unstable man on the British throne. He viewed Spain as a dying power, its rulers as clay in the hands of the upstart Bonaparte.

Astor, no less than Jefferson, thought in terms of western expansion, but where Jefferson was a dreamer and solicitous of public improvement, Astor was a cold realist and concerned only with the welfare of a fur merchant named Astor who had been born in Waldorf, Germany, on July 17, 1763.

The economic progress of the United States, in Astor's estimation, could come only with drastic and immense territorial changes. He gave his support to Jefferson's proposal to purchase West Florida and New Orleans from France, although he considered the move inade-

Washington Irving, *Astoria,* Philadelphia, 1836, and reprints; Gustavus Myers, *History of the Great American Fortunes,* Chicago, 1910; Phillips, *Fur Trade;* Maude A. Resecker, *The Oregon Trail and Some of its Blazers,* New York, 1930; Robert Stuart, *Discovery of the Oregon Trail,* ed. by P. A. Rollins, New York, 1935; Kenneth A. Spaulding, ed., *On the Oregon Trail: Robert Stuart's Journey of Discovery,* Norman, Okla., 1953; Bancroft, *Washington, Idaho and Montana;* Charles H. Carey, *History of the Pacific Northwest,* New York, 1931; David Lavender, *Land of Giants,* New York, 1958, and *Westward Vision,* New York, 1963; W. J. Ghent, *The Road to Oregon,* New York, 1929; Alexander Ross, *Adventures of the First Settlers on the Oregon . . . ,* London, 1849, Cleveland, 1904, and *Fur Hunters of the Far West,* London, 1855, and reprints; Gabriel Franchere, *Narrative of a Voyage to the Northwest Coast of America,* New York, 1854; Ross Cox, *Adventures on the Columbia River,* 2 vols., London, 1831.

quate, no more than a short step in the right direction. It would bring neither the needed security nor the desired opportunities for commercial exploitation.

If such prominent, prosperous, and well-informed men as De Witt Clinton and Gouvernor Morris considered the former butcher boy socially impossible, they held him in high esteem as a businessman, acknowledged his financial genius, and envied his rapidly accumulating fortunes. Astor complained not at all about the social barriers they erected against him, kept in close touch with them, and fully appreciated the value of their reports on the trend of matters in Washington. They were very useful as pipelines to high offices, and, even more important to him, they were not averse to spilling intelligence – confidentially, of course – in exchange for information on financial transactions and prospective business deals. Supplying such things was hardly a strain on Astor. He could have directed any man he favored to a road with highly profitable turnings.

It was from Clinton or Morris – probably from both of them – that Astor first learned of Napoleon's changing attitude toward the great Territory of Louisiana. At one time, Napoleon had made no secret of his ambition to reestablish a French colonial empire in America. However, the failure of his army to reconquer Santo Domingo, combined with the ominous turn of events in Europe, had relegated Louisiana to a position of diminishing importance in his thinking.

Astor promptly advanced an incredible scheme. He proposed to Clinton and Morris that they form a syndicate with him to buy the entire Territory of Louisiana and sell it to the United States. Profits from such a venture, as Astor envisioned them, could be expected to reach the stupendous total of $30,000,000. If Clinton and Morris considered Astor's scheme feasible, they were too slow in reaching a decision.

For six years after the size of the United States had been more than doubled by the purchase of Louisiana, Astor worked patiently and cautiously on his master plan. He gave to it the characteristics of a carefully programmed dynasty. Not only would fiscal marriages be arranged, they would be rigidly supervised. His American Fur Company would be the founder of the line, and its offspring, even though they might have no outward resemblance to their progenitor, the nature and qualities of the original blood would be predominant.

By 1809, he had decided that the first principality of the planned western empire would be established on the Northwest Pacific coast. A new scion of the line, the Pacific Fur Company, would rule over it.

Astor knew where to obtain the experienced lieutenants he needed. He went first to Montreal, talked with the men he wanted, and left the fur companies there and the Canadian government in a state of agitation. It was clearly apparent now that his plans were a serious menace to Canada's own prospects in the Far West.

Back in New York, Astor got in touch with several other men whom he knew either personally or by reputation, and who had been engaged in fur-trading ventures on the Missouri River. St. Louis fur traders had been alerted to the possibility of an invasion by Astor the previous year, when the American Fur Company had been chartered. Then Jefferson had written the governor of Louisiana Territory, the famed Meriwether Lewis, that a powerful company had been organized to carry on the Indian trade in the West on a large scale, with the intention of securing for the United States "exclusive possession" of that commerce. The president added that the new American company would be "under the direction of a most excellent man, a mr Astor mercht., of New York, long engaged in the business & perfectly master of it." Lewis had given this intelligence to the St. Louis traders, who had received it with something less than enthusiasm. Now the western fur trade, like the Canadian companies, could view with alarm the approach of the indomitable New Yorker, whose victories already had demonstrated that he was without a peer and whose resources appeared to be without limit.

All appearances of the situation gave rise to the conviction that a trade war would soon be raging on the Missouri, and the westerners girded themselves to meet the challenger. Astor fooled them. He had no intention of entering directly into the fur trade anywhere east of the Rocky Mountains. The war the westerners expected would come in time. Meanwhile, he was gazing far beyond the sources of the plains rivers, far beyond to other headwaters, to those which formed the Columbia system and emptied into the ocean that beat against the western rim of the continent.

Astor was going west, far west, and so American enterprise was being pushed from one ocean to the other, across the wilderness of the new America. The stakes were beyond imagination, and Montreal and Washington studied the situation and closely watched every move made. Not only the development of new business was involved. This meant a sharp turning in the political road. It prompted questions of boundaries and jurisdiction and sovereign rights that kept statesmen awake nights, and it conjured up dreadful pictures of conflict, not of the trade kind, but of bloodshed and death through the clash of international forces. Expansion was wonderful to contemplate, but not all the changes it would bring to the West necessarily would be beneficial. They might well be destructive and deleterious to the national welfare. There was a haze partially obscuring the brightness of the western sun.

In simple terms, Astor had one goal: to take over the American Northwest for himself. If the thought of helping the United States to develop its most remote territory entered his mind, he kept it a secret. To harbor such a thought longer than the time necessary to kill it would not have been in keeping with Astor's character. He despised nothing as much as public spirited citizens or government officials who sincerely struggled to improve the national welfare.

In June 1809, Astor brought his lieutenants together in New York, and they affixed their signatures to a contract that gave full evidence of his basic intentions. His incontestable strength was revealed throughout the thirty articles comprising the agreement. He, and he alone, was to manage all the business of the Pacific Fur Company, give all the orders, and authorize all actions, including expenditures. He was to advance all necessary funds, but he placed an initial limit of $400,000 on these. For the first five years, he was to bear all losses. This was a shrewd provision, for it augmented the means by which he would retain absolute control of the company.

No one could contest him if he decided that conditions did not warrant an expenditure. No one could say that he was obligated to chance a possible loss.

A hundred shares of stock would be issued, and profits would be divided according to the number of shares held by each partner. However, Astor would hold fifty shares himself, and fifteen more would be reserved for the use of the company. Any one of the fifteen shares could be issued to a good friend or even a member of the Astor family, should the company so decree, and the company was Astor. So it was possible for him to control sixty-five of the hundred shares.

As an additional safety precaution, he retained the privilege of making all his shares over to the American Fur Company, the parent corporation, under certain conditions, none of which appeared insuperable. The lifetime of the Pacific Fur Company was set at twenty years, but after the first five years all losses as well as profits would be borne proportionately by shareholders.

Astor divided the remaining thirty-five shares among his partners in this way: Alexander McKay, Donald McKenzie, Duncan McDougal, David Stuart, Wilson Price Hunt and Ramsay Crooks each received five shares. Robert McClellan and Joseph Miller were given two and one-half shares each.[2]

This was completely an undertaking of private capital, but was of vital importance to the course and the program of the national government, indeed, to every citizen and especially to those who resided west of the Mississippi River. Its boldness was no greater than its

---

[2] At a later date Robert Stuart would acquire a part of the share of David Stuart, who was his uncle.

significance. Its vitality could not then, and could not afterward, be overemphasized. In a very real sense, Astor would be the government in the Northwest, for the Federal government was not strong enough to perform what, by every legal definition, was its rightful function. Astor had appointed himself arbiter of any international disputes which might arise. He alone would be the antagonist of any foreign power which made an attempt to acquire legally or through piratical actions a portion of the potential riches of that vast and untouched empire.

Astor's plan called for the dispatch of two expeditions to the Northwest coast. One was to go overland from St. Louis, following the route of Lewis and Clark. Once on Pacific waters, it would trap and select sites for trading posts. The other was to go by sea from New York around Cape Horn in a vessel fully equipped and supplied for trade with Indians and for establishing not only a trading post but a strong fort near the mouth of the Columbia River. The name of the installation would be Astoria.

From the very moment the *Tonquin* sailed from New York harbor, the expedition by sea was doomed. From the very moment the keelboats pushed away from the St. Louis waterfront the overland Astorians were on a trail to failure.

It was as if all the forces of man and nature had combined to defeat and destroy the greatest project of the kind ever launched on American soil. The machinations of rivals, the political issues of the time, the geography, the climatic conditions, the perils of the wilderness were not responsible, either singly or in concert, for the debacle that resulted. Each of them contributed adverse turnings, but to these must be added individual weakness, greed, selfishness, venality, stupidity, dishonesty and hypocrisy – qualities as inherent and as powerful in men as those directly antithetical.

The *Tonquin,* carrying partners who were already disloyal to Astor, and commanded by a fool, sailed from New York on September 8, 1810. She was a fine ship, of three hundred tons, mounting twelve guns, and carrying a crew of twenty-one. With Captain Jonathan Thorn, a veteran naval officer, on the bridge, she undoubtedly would have given a good account of herself. Astor, however, had no intention of giving Thorn an opportunity to demonstrate his ability as a seafighter. He arranged with Washington to have the U. S. Frigate *Constitution* escort the *Tonquin* down the coast.

The partners on the *Tonquin* were McKay, McDougal and David and Robert Stuart. With them were eleven clerks, thirteen Canadian *voyageurs* and five mechanics. Before sailing, McKay and McDougal had called on the British minister. They disclosed the full plans of the Pacific Fur Company, details of its equipment and personnel, and asked for instructions to be followed in case of a war between the United States and England.

Numerous adjectives were used to describe Captain Thorn by his passengers, but if each was applicable, none was complimentary. He displayed a pathetic ignorance and a complete lack of understanding of the enormous scope and importance of the Astoria venture. Every view he held was limited to the confines of his ship; anything beyond that small world was out of his sphere, and therefore of no moment. Anything that interfered with his routine duties, even a passing thought or a casual word, infuriated him.

He stared down from the quarter-deck on his passengers with surly contempt, seeing them as unkempt braggarts, undisciplined backwoodsmen who would sit down to a stew of dog with filthy Indians, as disgusting landlubbers without property or pride who were living at the expense of a rich man. Thorn lumped partners, clerks, *voyageurs,* and mechanics together on a single low level. He refused to associate socially with the partners, even though they actually were part owners of the vessel, but he disdained even to speak in a friendly manner to the clerks, choosing to ignore the fact that all of them were young men of good families whose positions in society might well be above a level he could attain.

Bitterness, hatred, resentment and hostility which on several occasions reached a point of violence, continued throughout the miserable voyage of more than six months. It was on March 22, 1811, that the mouth of the Columbia was sighted. Here Thorn branded himself forever as an unconscionable and incompetent commander.

Fully aware of the navigational dangers in the wild and tempestuous entrance to the great river of the West, Thorn ordered five men, the first mate, one able seaman and three *voyageurs,* to take a whaleboat and find a passage for the ship. The Columbia was in vicious spring flood against the incoming tide. No one but a madman would have attempted to sound for a channel in the raging waters. Thorn was that madman. The five men rowed into the mists. They were never seen again.

Appearing unconcerned by the loss, Thorn ordered

a second boat out the next morning. It found no channel and had several close brushes with disaster before it could return. Undaunted, Thorn sent out a third boat, but it could accomplish nothing and was almost capsized by breakers. Disgusted and furious, Thorn sent out a fourth boat containing an officer, two white seamen and two Sandwich Islanders. It, too, vanished.

During the night the *Tonquin* nearly drifted to destruction on rocky reefs, but at daylight the weather improved, and with a strong flood tide and a favorable wind, she crossed the bar after scraping her keel several times. Shore parties immediately began to search for the missing men. They found two of the seamen. The other eight had perished.

Now Thorn demanded that the site for the fort be selected at once. When the traders, who knew the importance of locating in a strategic place, did not act fast enough to suit him, he ordered a shed erected on shore. As soon as it was ready, he began to move merchandise and equipment into it. By this arbitrary action, he forced the partners to settle on a site they considered unsatisfactory in several respects.

Thorn had kept on board a large manifest of goods to be used in trading with Indians along the coast. He waited only until the foundations of the fort were in place before sailing on this mission. McKay, wise in the ways of the red people and a veteran of the fur trade, sailed as supercargo. Shortly after the middle of May, the anchor of the *Tonquin* was dropped in Nootka Sound against the advice of the interpreter, Lamazee, who warned that the natives in the area were treacherous and hated white men. Thorn scoffed at the thought.

Trade goods were spread about the deck, and Thorn, making light of repeated warnings, permitted scores of Indians to board the ship. He demanded that his offers for their skins be accepted, and when the Indians insisted on bargaining, he drove them off in fury.

Early the next morning, the Indians returned in greater numbers. McKay protested against permitting so many of them on the deck at one time. The Indians carried no visible arms, but the interpreter expressed the belief they were concealing weapons beneath the mantles of skins they wore. As the Indians continued to pour over the rail, concern began to show in Thorn's face. He ordered some seamen aloft to make sail, and told others to weigh the anchor.

He had waited too long. As if at a silent signal, knives and hatchets appeared, and the Indians fell upon the white men. Within a few minutes, Thorn, McKay, and sixteen members of the crew were butchered. They all died leaving slain Indians scattered over the blood-smeared deck. Five crewmen, among them the badly wounded ship's clerk, Mr. Lewis, had managed to barricade themselves in a cabin. There they held out for the remainder of the day and through the night.

At dawn, Mr. Lewis cautiously crept out and found the ship deserted. Its partially raised anchor had caught, and the *Tonquin* floated serenely on smooth water. Several canoes filled with Indians were circling nearby, and Mr. Lewis signaled to them to come aboard, making signs of welcome and peace. Then he fled from sight.

The deck was soon crowded once again with Indians. The interpreter was with them. They began to poke cautiously into the interior of their prize. Suddenly the

Tonquin was lifted out of the water by a tremendous explosion.

Washington Irving, who had access to the Pacific Fur Company reports, wrote:

> Arms, legs and mutilated bodies were blown into the air, and dreadful havoc was made in the surrounding canoes. The interpreter was in the main chains at the time of the explosion, and was thrown unhurt into the water. . . According to his statement, the bay presented an awful spectacle after the catastrophe. The ship had disappeared. . . Upwards of a hundred savages were destroyed   .   .   .   many more shockingly mutilated, and for days afterward the limbs and bodies of the slain were thrown upon the beach.

It was the interpreter who reported how four of the five men barricaded in the cabin had slipped away from the ship under cover of darkness in a small boat. Mr. Lewis, knowing he could not live long, had refused to go with them. The four crewmen had been captured and tortured to death. Obviously, Mr. Lewis, his own life seeping away, had fired the ship's magazine.

"Such," Irving said, "is the melancholy story of the *Tonquin*."

The stories of the overland expedition and of Astoria itself, if not as bloody, are hardly less "melancholy."

In the later summer of 1810, Wilson Price Hunt arrived in St. Louis from Montreal with the nucleus of the overlanders – thirty Canadian *voyageurs* and the partners, McKenzie and Crooks. Miller was waiting for them. After considerable difficulty more *voyageurs* and hunters were enlisted, and boats, equipment and supplies were obtained.

Fall was at hand and within a few weeks the upper Missouri would be closed by ice, but Hunt was determined to avoid the expense and trouble of wintering the expedition in St. Louis. He announced they would push up the river as far as possible before cold weather halted them, after which they would establish winter quarters. The decision was a mistake. Months of discomfort, isolation and dreary quarters brought serious dissension. Minor grievances took on the proportions of major quarrels. Morale sank to a low level, and it appeared for a time that the company might break up.

The departure from St. Louis had been made on October 21, and for the next four weeks the heavy keel boats had been paddled, poled and hauled up the river. In that time, due to the expertness and unceasing hard work of the *voyageurs,* about 450 miles were traveled. On November 16, the mouth of a small creek, the Nadowa, was reached. Hunt decided that it was a suitable place to stop. Construction of log and earth shelters was begun. The halt had been made none too soon, for on the second day after their arrival at Nadowa Creek the river was choked with ice.

Hunt went back to St. Louis by horseback to report to Astor. He purchased another boat, recruited more men and engaged the noted Sioux interpreter, Pierre Dorion. Two distinguished passengers were on the boat as it ascended the river in the early spring. Hunt had agreed to transport them as far as the Mandans, and they were the first scientists to travel in the upper Missouri wilderness — John Bradbury, a naturalist sent out by the Linnean Society of Liverpool, and Thomas Nuttall, a botanist and writer. Both would leave to posterity papers of great historical value.

The winter headquarters at Nadowa Creek were reached April 17, and four days later the entire expedition pushed out into the raging current of the Missouri. Their destination on the Columbia was still more than three thousand miles away.

Late in May, five fur hunters were encountered whose names were to be permanently inscribed on the roster of the most intrepid Mountain Men. They were Alexander Carson, Ben Jones, John Hoback, Edward Robinson and Jacob Rezner. During the previous year they had been on the upper Missouri, and they were returning to St. Louis, but Hunt induced them to turn about and go with him to the Pacific.

Hunt had intended to follow the Missouri and Yellowstone rivers to the mountains, but the quintet of experienced Mountain Men urged him not to expose the company to the Blackfeet. They advised him to strike westward from the Arikara Villages,[3] and from that point make the entire journey to Columbia waters by land.

The Arikara Villages were reached on June 12. Hunt accepted the advice of the five men and began to trade for horses. More than a month was consumed by this task, and even though he had not obtained all the horses he wanted, Hunt ordered that the start westward be made.

On July 17, the Astorians set out across the vast plains. In the long file winding its way out of the valley of the Missouri were sixty-one men, one squaw and two small children.

Eighty-two horses had been obtained. Riding were the partners—Hunt, McKenzie, McKay, Crooks, Miller,

---

[3] Near Mobridge, South Dakota.

McClellan. Dorion, the intrepreter, his squaw and two children had been assigned two mounts. The others all walked, for the remaining seventy-four animals were heavily loaded with supplies.

In the truest sense, the company was breaking trail. They were taking a route to the mountains that no other American known to history had taken. The brothers Verendryes had crossed part of it more than a century before as they followed their great circular course, but this factor was of no value whatsoever to the Astorians. Nor were there any records, or even word-of-mouth reports, to aid them. It is known they met Cheyennes early in August, for they obtained thirty-six more horses from them. Probably they encountered some traveling Sioux, and it is certain they met Crows. They passed through the heart of Absaroka, the homeland of that tribe.

Indians would have informed them of the nature of the country ahead and directed them to streams, but even with this assistance they would have needed to rely on the uncanny ability of the Mountain Men to locate the most advantageous routes. When they reached Wind River on September 9, they were in country which had been well explored.

Union Pass opened a way for them. On September 26, they stood on the bank of a fine grey-green river. It was the Snake, and its water reached the Columbia, but where or how far ahead of them lay that confluence they had no idea.

The *voyageurs,* weary of the long journey over dry land, danced with joy at the sight of the strong swift stream. *Au revoir, aux chevaux!* Floating down the Snake would be dreaming. Here we come, Columbia!

However, the Indians who came into the company's camp shook their heads gravely when canoe travel was mentioned. It was not possible, they said, for the river was deceitful. The *voyageurs* roared – the stupid Indians did not know how well they handle canoes. White water was nothing to them.

Hunt's mistake was not in failing to carry out his orders, but in failing to heed the admonitions of the Indians.

The company was now on Pacific waters, and so it had reached territory in which Pacific Fur Company operations were to be conducted. Two contingents were detached to trap. They would remain in the Snake country through the winter and spring, and would bring their catches to the Columbia the following summer. Perhaps if Hunt had known what obstacles lay between him and the Columbia, he would not have given so much thought to business.

In one of the parties remaining, were Alexander Carson, Pierre Delauney, Pierre Detaye, and one St. Michael. In the other were John Hoback, Edward Robinson, Jacob Rezner, and a hunter named Cass. Suddenly, the partner Joseph Miller announced that he, too, would remain behind. In a fit of wild rage he signed away his company shares. He was, he declared, disgusted with the whole operation, and would become a plain trapper. The other partners, mystified by his violent act, regretfully agreed to leave him behind.

On October 19, the expedition started down the Snake in fifteen canoes which the *voyageurs* had constructed. For nine days they sped on, shouting their delight and ecstacy, borne on the powerful shoulders of the magnificent stream. Then, suddenly, the true character of the Snake, so appropriately named, was revealed to them in all its horror. Canoes were torn apart. A *voyageur* was drowned. They had reached the impassable Cauldron Linn. Several days of reconnoitering told them further travel by water was impossible. There was only one way out – by the faint animal trails that wound away through the tortured country.

The journey of the Astorians from the Cauldron Linn to the mouth of the Columbia was one of desperation, hopelessness, sickness, injury, tortuous hunger and death. The company became divided into several bands. A *voyageur* vanished. Dorion's wife gave birth to a child that lived only a few days. Three men abandoned the struggle and went to live with Indians. Another collapsed and had to be left in an Indian village. All resembled walking skeletons, surviving on dog, ground squirrels and beaver as they fought their ways through the mountains toward the great river.

It was not until January 18, 1812, that the first of them, led by McKenzie and McClellan, reached Astoria. Nearly a month later, Hunt and his men staggered in. Not until May were the last two overlanders, Crooks and Day, found on the upper Columbia by a trapping party out of Astoria. They were nearly dead from exposure and hunger.

The story of Astoria from that time on is one of futility, deceit and disloyalty. While trapping operations on the upper river were comparatively successful, both McClellan and Crooks saw no future for them in the company, and they gave up their shares, as Miller had done.

In the summer of 1812, trapping contingents were sent out, posts were established, and Robert Stuart started east with reports for Astor. At that time the men on the Columbia and the great trader in New York had been separated, not only by thousands of miles but by a gulf of silence two years in width.

The partners at Astoria, especially the traitorous McDougal, had good reason to wonder if war had started between England and America. Canadians were in the Columbia country. Indeed, when construction of the fort at Astoria was begun, a contingent from the North West Company had been camped only thirty miles up the river. The Astor company had won the race for the strategic site only by that narrow margin. Other Canadians had arrived since. Well might the Astorians wonder if they could hold their ground under the conditions of war. As far as they knew, the ownership of Oregon had never been settled. It belonged to those strong enough to occupy it. A single British or American warship might be the deciding factor.

McKenzie was on the Spokane River in December 1812, when John George McTavish and a strong company of North West Company men arrived from the east and answered the question uppermost in the minds of the Astorians. McTavish brought word that England and the United States were at war. McKenzie raced down river to Astoria with the news.

He and McDougal quickly put their heads together to decide on a course. The two Scots not unhappily came to the conclusion that the British navy would prevent Astor from sending any ships to the Columbia. With supplies running low, Astoria would have to be abandoned not later than the coming summer.

Astoria was doomed.

McDougal had known all along what he would do under such circumstances, and when the time came he did it. He sold Astoria to the North West Company for $58,291.02. A reasonable price would have been $200,000. The furs on hand alone were worth a $100,000 at the mouth of the Columbia. In Canton or London they would have brought at least four times that amount.

It was evident that John George McTavish had not led his brigade across the continent to attempt to take Astoria by force of arms, although he might well have done that without great difficulty. Perhaps the remark that the partners of the North West Company were in the main men who preferred orthodox methods to banditry is irrelevant. They were not guided by gentlemanly instincts in their negotiations at Astoria, but by practicality and good sense. They understood the power of Astor. Starting a shooting war with him would have gained them nothing that a few dollars could not gain. Violence on the Columbia might well have brought retaliation in kind on their posts east of the mountains, along the international border and in the Great Lakes region. They might win a small battle and lose a war.

It was quite enough to have their country under attack by the United States without having a private army of Astor shooting at them. Under such circumstances, in the event of a British capitulation their business position would be disastrous. As far as bringing the Northwest coast under their flag was concerned, that was really not a conquest they needed to consider. In the first place, they were merchants and traders, not soldiers. In the second place, the British navy was on the way, and territorial acquisition was properly its job. In fact, Mc-Tavish carried a letter he had received from an uncle which said that a British frigate was en route "to destroy everything that is American on the N. W. Coast."

The expected British warship arrived in November 1813. She was the *Racoon,* mounting twenty-six guns. Captain Black landed and enjoyed a good dinner at the fort, but he was unable to conceal his disappointment. He had been led to believe that a valuable prize awaited capture on the Columbia. All he found was a cluster of huts surrounded by a stockade, and a group of dirty Indians lounging at the gate. This disreputable conglomeration of hovels was what he had been sent halfway around the world to take. "Damn!" he growled.

He had not needed to be disappointed or ashamed. In taking possession of Astoria, he had saved a western empire for his country.

It remains to be recounted that when Astoria fell, Robert Stuart and six companions were deep in the western wilderness, en route to St. Louis with dispatches for Astor. They would know nothing of the events on the Columbia until long after they had reached civilization.

With Stuart were Crooks, McClellan, Miller, and three hunters, Andri Vallar, Ben Jones and Francis Leclerc.

Theirs was an incredible journey. They traveled 3,768 miles from Astoria to St. Louis, taking 306 days. They suffered severe and prolonged hardships, and several times nearly died from exposure and hunger.

It was also an epic journey, an achievement of the greatest significance, in the truest sense a bona fide trip of discovery. Robert Stuart and his companions were the first to find a route from the Pacific to the Missouri River that could be traversed by wagons.

The Astoria dream had been crushed, yet disaster was not alone its hallmark. It brought accomplishments of a new kind. It left monuments for the nation to see along its earthly course. Even more important, it left flags waving in the imaginations and the thoughts of Americans, it opened their eyes to new visions and new vistas greater than any they had ever known – it turned their faces toward far-off Oregon.

1817

TURNING NUMBER THREE

———◆———

A Strange New Voice
of Hope and Doom

The steamboat reaches the Missouri River
and revolutionizes western commerce

III

A Strange New Voice
of Hope and Doom

. . . less than two years ago, the first steamboat arrived in St. Louis. We hailed it as the day of small things, but the glorious consummation of all our wishes is daily arriving. . . Who could or would have dared to conjecture that in 1819 we should have the arrival of a steamboat from Philadelphia or New York? Yet such is the fact!

As he wrote those words, the editor of the *Missouri Gazette* was no more astounded than any other person who had the intelligence to realize the significance of the change which had taken place.

The first steamboat whistle ever heard in St. Louis startled the people on the sultry afternoon of August 2, 1817. From offices, saloons, shops and residences they ran into the streets, voicing their excitement, staring in wonder toward the waterfront. They saw in reality what they had hesitated to believe had happened.

They saw the tall stacks, the smoke, the flying sparks, the frothing wake of the *Zebulon M. Pike* as it bucked the current to swing into the levee. The wild shouting of men, the shrill cries of women and children, the noise of shots answered the whistle. Drivers struggled to control plunging horses. Dogs slunk away to find safety. In the eyes of Indians was a look of mingled fear and consternation.

It was not only a day for celebration, as Bishop Du Bourg understood, but a day to be thankful, for God had seen fit to bestow upon Missouri the benefit of man's ingenuity. The bishop could pray that the new way of life which had come so suddenly to the wilderness would inspire in all peoples – red, white and black – greater goodness and reverence, but he would be disappointed.

The entire change from the age of paddle and pole to the age of steam had occurred within the memory of the young. They could remember the steps, taken both up and down the rivers, which had linked the wilderness and the civilized world by an indestructible bond made of fire and water and iron.

The mackinaws, the barges, the broadhorns, the arks and the keelboats had gone down the rivers since the first forts were established. Only the keelboats had come up, the strength of human muscles defying and conquering the gravity of the waters.

Then, in 1792, on the upper Ohio, ingenious men had devised a means of avoiding the expense of transferring goods from river craft to sailing vessels at New Orleans. They constructed ships that could ride the current to the sea, then raise their sails for an ocean crossing.[1]

One of the first of these ships went directly to Leghorn, Italy, with a cargo of hemp, tobacco and cotton

---

[1] Billington, *Westward Expansion;* Phillip E. Chappell, *History of the Missouri River,* Kansas City, 1905; Emerson W. Gould, *Fifty Years on the Mississippi,* St. Louis, 1889; H. M. Chittenden, *History of Early Steamboat Navigation on the Missouri River: Life and Adventure of Joseph LaBarge,* New York, 1903; Chittenden, *Life . . . of de Smet.*

from Kentucky and Tennessee, but when its captain presented papers showing he had cleared from Pittsburg, they were refused. There was no such port. The captain produced a map of the United States, guided the eyes of Italian officials up the Mississippi for a thousand miles, up the Ohio for another thousand. There was a Pittsburgh. The Italians would have been no more astonished if he had guided them to the moon.

Down the Ohio and the Mississippi, not only from the building ways of Pittsburgh, but from those in Marietta, Wheeling and Louisville, went the sailing ships to Europe, to the West Indies, to the cities of the Atlantic coast. They were true deep water ships, as large as those built in New York or Boston or Philedalphia. In the year of the Louisiana Purchase there were vessels of 250 tons burthen and larger moving downstream to the Gulf of Mexico. Of course, none of those which sailed between the years 1792 and 1811 ever came back, but that was a disadvantage that was suddenly eliminated.

In 1811, Nicholas J. Roosevelt, a colleague of the inventor, Robert Fulton, and of the noted diplomat, Robert R. Livingston, superintended the building and launching of the steamboat, *New Orleans,* at Pittsburgh. One editor spoke of him as "Mr. Roosevelt, an enterprising man," and remarked that it would be "as pleasing as novel to see a huge boat working her way up the windings of the Ohio . . . moving within the secrets of her own wonderful mechanism, and propelled by power undiscoverable. This plan if it succeeds must open to view flattering prospects to an immense country . . ."

The plan would succeed.

The *New Orleans* never returned to its home, but some of her relatives came upstream, and if the water was high enough they passed the rapids at Louisville.

"How do the rivers and canals of the old world dwindle to insignificance compared with this!" cried the *Niles Register*. The "old world" had then been gone only five years, but the way of the new was incomparably swift. Time, and so life itself, seemed to pass with greater celerity now.

There were twenty steamboats fighting the Ohio in that summer of 1817 when the *Pike,* instead of turning into it, continued on up the Mississippi, with every revolution of its paddle wheels giving new direction to the destiny of the West.

The mouth of the Missouri was only "two whistle blasts" beyond the St. Louis levee, but the captains shook their heads at the mighty brown flood, and went on up the gentler Mississippi. They wanted none of that mad river from the unknown, and the men of the keelboats thought they understood. They might pull and push and row and curse the keelboats up the Missouri, avoiding the snags and drift logs and bars, but the steamboat had no such maneuverability. Power wasn't everything. It was doubtful that the steamboat would ever supplant the keelboat on the Missouri.

As they were soon to learn, they were poor prophets. The editor of the *Gazette* had no more than printed his exclamation about ships from New York docking at St. Louis than the steamboat *Independence* tied up at Franklin, 205 miles above the Missouri's mouth. A wildly excited crowd shouted *bon voyage* as it went on a few miles more to Chariton. There it turned back to St. Louis.

The round trip had been accomplished in only twenty-one days.

If the obituary of the keelboat had been written, even set in type, it was far from dead. If the fur traders could believe its days were numbered, they had no time to dwell on the matter. Moreover, in view of the rapidity with which events had transpired in the immediate past, a man would be foolish to predict what would happen in the immediate future. It was the moment at hand to which they must give their full attention, the pressing important problems before them and which they must resolve without delay.

The situation was not difficult to understand, even though it continued to be astonishing. As it had been only yesterday, a keelboat would leave New Orleans in March, and the summer would be giving way to fall before its cargo would be unloaded at St. Louis. That was too late in the season for the goods to be sent on up the Missouri, for the river would be closed by ice before the upper reaches could be reached. The merchandise which was moved into St. Louis warehouses in August or September would have been ordered the previous year, and it would not arrive on the upper Missouri until late in the summer of the next year.

At the outset, the steamboat had cut this time schedule by at least twelve months. If a steamboat left New Orleans in March, it reached St. Louis in time for its cargo to be transferred to keelboats and sent immediately up the river. The companies seldom left before late April or early May, and it was even possible to start in June and get to the farthest posts before snow fell.

Time was not the only thing that could be saved. An amazingly large tonnage, all a trading house would need for an entire season, as well as horses, wagons and livestock, could be transported on even a small steamboat. Both inventories and the costs resulting from long storage were decreased. As the number of steamboats plying the Mississippi increased – and they increased rapidly from the beginning – freight charges went down, bringing additional savings. For what one boat could do, others could do, and with competition came rivalry in providing good service and a struggle to secure business.

Seemingly almost overnight, all business thinking, all planning – the entire system of the fur trade – had to be revised.

The traders had no more than begun to accomplish these tasks before steamboat whistles blew at the mouth of the Kansas, upstream four hundred miles from St. Louis, then at Fort Leavenworth, and in the fall of 1819 came news that was almost unbelievable. The *Independence,* built for the United States army, had reached the Council Bluffs, above the mouth of the Platte.

Once again all outlooks were changed, all programs had to be reconsidered, new systems had to be devised.

Could they go farther? Could they go all the way?

Not only the unpredictable character of the river, but the machinations and stupidity, the illusions and greed, of men would write the answers to those questions, and the answers would be long in coming, but the fur traders would never stop thinking about them, wondering what they would be.

The Council Bluffs was more than far enough up the Missouri to let the Indians realize that a monster more formdiable, more awesome and fearful, more foreboding, than the wildest imagination could create had come among them.

It was a thing beyond the realm of dreams, not only inexplicable but inconceivable. The powers of the manitous had been usurped. No – medicine as strong had never been possessed by any god. With confounding ease the fireboat overcame the strength of the river. Its voice sent wild game fleeing in panic across the prairies. Sparks it belched at the sky were obediently carried by the wind to start grass fires. Its lofty twin chimneys poured out clouds of smoke, but they were signals that were beyond comprehension.

Word of the wonder sped up the river, for beyond the Council Bluffs, far beyond the Mandans, striking those who had never seen it with consternation and terror. Traders who were up there on the far upper rivers brought back to St. Louis amusing intelligence, and the *Republican* reported with understandable satisfaction that respect for Americans was on the rise in all the Indian country. It was the expressed view of several prominent chiefs that the British, who never ceased attempts to poison the Indians against the Americans, henceforth would be wise to lock their tongues. The British had produced no such miracle, and they might do well if they burned their canoes and trade goods, for it was unlikely they would have further use for them. It was obvious that no one could compete with the Americans.

The British had other ideas, but the Indians were not

to be caught failing to pay obeisance to the supernatural, and in this case the most potent medicine they had ever known. They would come to understand the fallacy in their thinking, and they would find renewed faith in their old gods and turn back to them. Meanwhile, to the traders of St. Louis, the news of the Indians' fears would be as encouraging as it was satisfying and amusing.

The first boats were sidewheelers, with a single engine and an immense flywheel. They were not practicable on the wild Missouri, but designers and engineers, learning from costly and tragic experiences, would soon eliminate the drawbacks.

Lengths would be more than doubled   .   .   .   from a hundred feet to more than two hundred feet   .   .   . while the draft was decreased. The first boats to turn up the Big Muddy needed more than six feet of water to clear their keel, yet they could carry only seventy-five to one hundred tons of cargo. Only a few years would pass before boats with flat bottoms would draw only fifty inches when loaded with five hundred tons. The balanced rudder had been invented, a rudder with a blade on each side of the rudder post, and this made the sternwheel practicable. Two engines, one on each side, communicated directly with the wheel shaft.

Still a boat frequently had to be pushed over sandbars, but the long poles of the old keelboats were supplanted by steam capstans and huge spars, and machine energy performed the toil instead of human backs. The steam did the work of loading and unloading, as well, the flesh and blood laborers being eliminated by powerful hoists. Automation came to the rivers, and one well might wonder what miracles the fabulous minds of engineers would accomplish before another trading season had passed.

The interiors were not forgotten, and luxury and comfort kept pace with the mechanical improvements. In addition to the bunk rooms for commonplace hunters and *voyageurs,* there were staterooms for the *bourgeois,* the partners, the army officers, the scientists. Class and position were recognized, and the degrees were reflected in fares, assignments to quarters, and positions at table.

Pork, lyed corn and navy beans were the standard menu in the beginning, and they were slopped out. The only variations were wild game. Hunters were carried, and they went ashore as meat was needed, returning with deer, antelope, buffalo in bloody quarters to cut up on the deck. The open air kitchens gave way to well-equipped galleys, and there were broiled and roasted meats, steamed vegetables, greens, pastries, palatable coffee, fruits, cheeses, wines. Cuisine and luxury not surpassed on any boats in the world would continue to improve until the last whistle sounded on the river, and was mocked by the throaty voice of the locomotive.

Father Pierre-Jean de Smet, making his many journeys to the Indian Country, had seen the changes takes place. He had known the crudeness and discomfort of the first boats, and he had known the floating palaces that followed them. Of one he wrote:

> Her crew consists of a captain, two clerks, two pilots and an assistant, two engineers, two mates, a steward, two watchmen, one head cook and two assistants, one *hotellier* (bartender), seven cabin boys, a porter or baggage man, eight deckhands (white), four firemen, nineteen negroes for all the work of the boat, and one chambermaid.

The main cabin consists of thirty staterooms, seven feet
long by six wide, and with two berths each. There are
thirty-two first class passengers, fifteen gentlemen, twelve
ladies and five children.

It was a typical Missouri River boat, a masterpiece of
scientific achievement carrying the amenities of civilization into a land that had not yet been conquered, a land
in which the howl of the wolf was echoed by the wild
cry of the warpath, and in which the thunder of the
heavens was repeated by the beating of savage drums.

"All the way" meant above the Yellowstone, above
the Musselshell, above the Marias, depending how imagi-
native a man was or how extreme his thinking. The
Yellowstone was far enough for most men, and their
answer to the question was *no*. They had good reasons
to believe as they did.

No one could be sure from one day to the next of the
location of the channel. "Of all the variable things in
creation," wrote the editor of the Sioux City *Register,*
"the most uncertain are the action of a jury, the state
of a woman's mind, and the condition of the Missouri
River." Here today was a bend, and here tomorrow was
a lake. The changing never ceased. Cliffs crumbled and
were absorbed by onrushing water, bearing its countless
millions of tons of the earth toward the far-off sea. Wide
forests were swallowed. The Mountain Men had given
to one area the name Devil's Rake. In it gigantic trees
lifted naked and menacing limbs from the water. The
limbs thrashed in the current, throwing up a foam with
a furious hissing sound.

The violence of the Missouri struck terror in the hearts of brave men. Father de Smet commented:

> I fear the sea, I will admit, but all the storms and other unpleasant things I have experienced in four different voyages did not inspire so much terror in me as the navigation of the somber, treacherous and muddy Missouri.
>
> Steam navigation on it is one of the most dangerous things a man can undertake. The current of this river is the swiftest; high pressure is therefore required to overcome it, and hence the continual danger to which the traveler is exposed of finding himself overturned, and even, as happens only too often, of having his limbs shattered and hurled here and there. . . Add the sandbars with which the river is filled, and upon which one is always being cast, and the inumerable snags and sawyers upon which boats are often wrecked; all these things brought us several times within a finger's breadth of our destruction.

The captains of the boats were in the public limelight. They were the great adventurers of the moment. The fabulous exploits of the John Colters and the Andrew Henrys and the Manuel Lisas were not forgotten, but the people also spoke in awe of the courageous feats of the pilots, of the Joseph La Barges and the Joseph Sires and the Jacques Desires.

The great river was a moving graveyard, and the monuments to the pilots who had gambled and lost stood on its banks. These were the wrecks of the boats driven on by the men who had defied the water and the wind, the current and the bars, to go farther or faster than their colleagues, to win glory and to make a dream come true.

Boilers burst, and a hundred bodies would be hurled with the shattered superstructure and hull into the air, and they would quickly disappear in the brown raging torrent. Whirlpools not known to exist were suddenly encountered. Boats were spun and drawn down to destruction. Submerged logs drove into a paddle wheel, and the crippled boat clung to the shore, awaiting the *coup de grace* that might come from a gale, a prairie fire, or more logs.

Vision and determination were not to be destroyed by failure and catastrophe, not even by death. "They can go all the way," some men said, and if they had no practical knowledge to support their contention, they held an indestructible conviction in their hearts.

Kenneth McKenzie was astute, haughty and bold. As chief of the Upper Missouri Outfit of Astor's American Fur Company, he ruled with supreme authority and iron discipline. His jurisdiction was all the immense territory of the upper Missouri River above the Platte. As progressive as he was courageous, from the time he assumed command of the great northern fur empire in 1827, he had urged that an attempt to take a steamboat as far as the mouth of the Yellowstone be made. By personal appeals and by letters he implored Ramsay Crooks and Pierre Chouteau, Jr., the Astor lieutenants in St. Louis, to undertake the venture, but they rejected the proposal as infeasible.

In the spring of 1830, he went again down the river from his headquarters at Fort Union to renew his efforts, and once again he found Crooks and Chouteau unreceptive to the idea. They labeled it impractical, if not impossible, arguing that the expense would be great, and that while there was sufficient water for steamboat navigation in the lower river, the bars, snags, rocks and narrow channels of the upper river made it a perilous and unpredictable gauntlet. Loss of a steamboat that was heavily loaded with furs and supplies might wipe out the profits of an entire season.

McKenzie was not to be dissuaded and continued to insist that the feat could be accomplished. Just because it had not been done, he argued, was a poor reason for refusing to try. Admittedly it would be hazardous, but if it succeeded profits would be increased. Fewer men would be needed, thus the payroll would be decreased. A small, powerful boat, one that was specially built for the attempt, would cost no more than a mere $7,000. It could leave St. Louis in April, after all ice was out of the lower river, and be back with the catch of the previous winter and the spring by the end of June.

Under such conditions, McKenzie pointed out, he could hold keelboats and barges up the river, and they could be sent down with furs late in the fall. They also would be available in case the steamboat met with an accident. As he saw the situation, the greatest problem would be a breakdown in the machinery far up the river, but that could be overcome by sending up spare parts and by establishing blacksmith shops at strategic points. If the American Fur Company did not carry out the scheme, he warned, someone else would beat them to it.

Crooks and Chouteau remained unconvinced and refused to approve the plan. McKenzie went back up the river to Fort Union, at the mouth of the Yellowstone, eighteen hundred miles above St. Louis, a dejected man. He was not aware that Chouteau had undergone a change of mind.

Soon after McKenzie had left St. Louis, Chouteau had written to Astor in New York advocating an attempt to take a steamboat to Fort Union. Chouteau's letter stated:

> . . . we have been contemplating the project of building a small steamboat for the trade of the upper Missouri. We believe that the navigation will be much safer in going up, and possibly also in coming down, than it is by keelboat. The only serious drawback will be the danger of breakage of some important pieces of machinery, which it would be difficult and perhaps impossible to repair on the spot. However, after consultation with some of the ablest steamboat captains, we think that by having spare sparts and a good blacksmith outfit on board, we may be able to overcome this difficulty. I imagine that there will always be a little risk to run, but I also believe that, if we succeed, it will be a great advantage to our business.

Continuing in the historic letter to voice McKenzie's contentions, Chouteau told Astor:

> The expenses we are annually put to in the purchase of keelboats and supplies, and in advances to *engages* before their departure, are enormous, and have to be repeated every year. With the steamboat, we could keep all our men in the Indian country, where we could pay the greater part of their wages in merchandise instead of making the large outlay of cash which we are now constantly required to do.

No argument could have been more appealing to Astor. It had always pained him greatly when he was obliged to pay wages in cash, and he had sought every means of paying them in merchandise. In this way he was able to make a profit of three hundred to four hundred per cent on clothes and equipment which his employees must have to survive in the wilderness. The oppressive evil system kept the employees of the company in virtual bondage, from which there was no escape, except by becoming renegades subject to severe legal penalties.

Chouteau's letter confidently continued:

> The boat would make the voyage to the upper river every spring. By starting from St. Louis at the beginning of April with the full season's outfit of merchandise, it would probably be back early in June, and bring with it a portion of the peltries. The finer furs could still be brought down in the ordinary way. The merchandise would all reach its destination before ice closed in the fall, which we now sometimes fail to do, to our great loss. Furthermore, by having boats on hand at the trading posts, we can always bring down the returns in case of accident to the steamboat. After the return of the latter from the annual trip it can be used in freighting on the lower river during the balance of the season. Such a boat as we require we think will cost in Cincinnati or Marietta about $7,000, but as we shall want a number of duplicate parts and extras the cost may amount to $8,000.

Whatever else Astor might have been, he was not timid. The danger of possible losses seldom influenced him against an enterprise that might increase business and profits. His approval of the steamboat plan came back to Chouteau by return mail.

Chouteau wasted no time, and by October 1830, he had arranged to have the boat constructed in Louisville. It was to be delivered to St. Louis by April 1, 1831, and its name, appropriately, would be the *Yellowstone*.

April 16, 1831, was a day for celebration on the St. Louis waterfront. Steamboat whistles shrieked. Guns were fired. Drinks flowed. A band played, and the crowd shouted and screamed and yelled against the music. The *Yellowstone* was starting for the river after which it had been named.

Men cursed John Jacob Astor's meanness and dishonest trade practices, while at the same time they praised his daring and enterprise. If his boat made it all the way, the economy of St. Louis would be given a great boost. Another new day would dawn for the fur trade, indeed for all business, a day which would bring advantages only a few far-seeing men, a few visionaries, had ever thought possible.

Sharing the pilot house with Captain B. Young as the sturdy little steamer plowed into the spring flood of the Missouri was a proud Pierre Chouteau. The shiny new *Yellowstone* was a thing of beauty. She was 130 feet long, had a nineteen-foot beam and a six-foot hold. Her specifications would be the model for other vessels that would follow her up the great highway to the wilderness: side wheel, single engine, flywheel, cabin aft of the shaft, ladies cabin in the stern hold, boiler decks open, no hurricane roof, pilothouse elevated, two smoke stacks, one rudder, six-foot wheel bucket, eighteen-foot wheel, landing stages aft, 4½ feet draft light, and 5½ feet when loaded with seventy-five tons of cargo.

For six weeks in that spring of 1831, the *Yellowstone* fought her way on against the mighty current, and on May 31 she passed the mouth of the Niobrara. History already had been made, for no steamboat had ever gone that far, but she did not pause to consider her laurels.

Then suddenly, as if resenting the defiance of its power, the river struck back. The water suddenly fell, and the *Yellowstone* was held fast on a bar.

Days passed. Each morning Pierre Chouteau, burning with impatience, profoundly aggravated, and fearing the great experiement was to fail, went ashore and paced back and forth on high ground, watching the brassy sky for signs of rain, muttering a prayer for more water. The others on the boat christened the site Chouteau's Bluffs, by which name it would always be known. At last, unable to contain himself longer and admitting defeat, he sent messengers upriver to Fort Tecumseh with orders to bring keelboats down to the stranded *Yellowstone*. They arrived in a few days, and enough of the cargo was taken off to allow the vessel to proceed on to the fort.

Chouteau dispatched a canoe down river with an express for Astor. *"Ce ne fut donc qu'a la faveur de trois berges, que j'envoyai chercher au Petit Missouri, et qui recurent une grande partie de la charge, qu'il m' a ete possible de me rendre avec le bateau le 19 Juin au Fort Tecumser,"* he wrote.

It was too late in the summer to go farther, but there were reasons for satisfaction and rejoicing. Although it had not reached its destination, the *Yellowstone* had demonstrated that steamboat traffic on the upper Missouri was practicable. Greater experience and knowledge of the river were needed, and they would be gained in time. Chouteau ordered the craft to turn back, convinced that another attempt would succeed. It would be made in the spring of 1832.

The *Yellowstone* traveled fast down the river, touching the wharf at St. Louis, to the accompaniment of more gunfire and whistle blowing, on July 15. She brought from Fort Tecumseh and other stations a full cargo of robes, furs, and ten thousand pounds of buffalo tongues.

American Fur Company Mountain Men coming into Fort Union in the spring and early summer of 1832 with their winter catches found the place in a state of wild excitement. From the first light of the dawn to the last vestige of the twilight lookouts in the bastions strained their eyes on the distant Missouri.

The *Yellowstone* had left St. Louis on March 26th. Pierre Chouteau was once more in the pilot house. Another passenger was the celebrated artist, George Catlin. To both of these men, but not for the same reasons, the heavily loaded, crowded little craft was a beautiful sight as she fought the muddy flood. Her lofty twin chimneys poured out clouds of wood smoke, writing in the sky which told of the beginning of a new age, a new destiny, for the West.

For nearly eight weeks she toiled before she stopped to rest. It was the last day of May when she reached Fort Tecumseh for the second time. Six days were given over to making repairs and cleaning the machinery. A new post was being erected there, and during the respite in the journey ceremonies were held and it was christened Fort Pierre.[2]

Leaving Fort Pierre on June 5, the *Yellowstone* struggled and pounded her way on upstream, advancing with every turn of her wheels upon water through which a steamboat had never passed. In the amazingly short time of twelve days it came in sight of the Fort Union lookouts.

The most modern mode of water travel on earth had reached the heart of the American West. The Missouri had been conquered by steam. Never again would men break their bodies toiling against the great river. In ten

---

[2] South Dakota.

weeks — with good luck — supplies and merchandise would reach the Yellowstone from St. Louis. In half that time, the furs would be brought back.

If it had been Astor's money which had made the great feat possible, it was to Kenneth McKenzie, who had always believed it could be accomplished and who had been the first to advocate the attempt, and to Pierre Chouteau, who had carried out the plan, that the credit belonged.

Chouteau received it. McKenzie was ignored. From New York Crooks wrote Chouteau:

> I congratulate you most cordially on your perseverence and ultimate success in reaching the Yellowstone by steam, and the future historian of the Missouri will preserve for you the honorable and enviable distinction of having accomplished an object of immense importance, by exhibiting the practicability of conquering the obstructions of the Missouri considered till almost the present day insurmountable to steamboats even among those best acquainted with their capabilities.
>
> *You have brought the falls of the Missouri as near, comparatively, as was the River Platte in my younger days.*

From Bellevue, France, Astor wrote Chouteau: "Your voyage in the *Yellowstone* attracted much attention in Europe, and has been noted in all the papers here."

Kenneth McKenzie, king of the upper river, did not resent the neglect. He was not as much interested in receiving personal congratulations as he was in learning what effect the arrival of the *Yellowstone* would have on the wild people who inhabited the immense empire over which he reigned.

What he saw was far more gratifying than any amount

of adulation from Astor. Indians, many of whom had
never before appeared at a white man's fort, had traveled
hundreds of miles to Fort Union to stare at the monster
which walked on the water. To them it was more than
an astonishing product of the Great White Father's magic.
It was a supernatural phenomenon beyond all possible
understanding. Their hearts were weighted with terror.

Long before the outside world had realized the full
meaning of the *Yellowstone's* accomplishment, McKenzie
had read the signs prognosticating the change that was
to come to the savage, boundless territory over which
ranged the Blackfeet, the Gros Ventres, the Assiniboines,
the Bloods, the Piegans, the Crows. He read the signs in
their faces, in their eyes, in their hushed words and their
gestures.

That day the *Yellowstone* had created a respect for
the Upper Missouri Outfit, and for him, that could not
have been won in a hundred years of giving presents and
smoking pipes about council fires.

McKenzie knew not only a greater gratification than
ever before, but he knew that he had obtained greater
power than he could have dreamed of possessing. He
strutted in his military uniform, with its polished belt
and holster, shiny metal buttons, silver and gold adornments, convinced that he could never be defeated, or
even bested, in the fur trade by either British or American
competitors. He was supreme, secure and untouchable.
Great days had come to his kingdom, and they would
make him fabulously rich.

At every post on the Missouri one day had suddenly
become more important than any other of the year,

Christmas not excluded. It was the day on which the annual steamboat arrived, a day to which everyone looked forward, to which all accounts, all transactions, all business was geared. But if it was the happiest day of the year, the day on which the annual boat turned back downstream was the saddest. Many years were to pass after the *Yellowstone* opened the water gateway to the Far West before the posts of the upper river saw more than one boat during a summer. And there were years when they waited in vain, when they heard no whistle.

Frequently the river claimed its bounty, inflicting profound disappointment, suffering and tragedy with impartial cruelty. Father de Smet could write from firsthand experience. In 1839 he was stationed at the crude little St. Joseph's Mission, in the country of the Potawatomies, above the Council Bluffs. On April 20 word spread swiftly from village to village that the first steamboat of the season from St. Louis was approaching.

During the last months of the winter a scarcity of game had reduced many of the Indians in the area to a diet of acorns and roots. Joyously they moved toward the landing to get the supplies from the government, which they knew would be aboard the steamer. No less relief was displayed at the mission, for there the larder was almost empty, and that end had been averted only by supplementing the few remaining staples with the same kinds of unpalatable food on which the Indians were subsisting. Father de Smet had been for several weeks without shoes, his last pair having disintegrated in the manner of snow in a spring thaw.

Without delay, and thinking of his suffering feet even more than his stomach, he followed two handcarts drawn by his ragged assistants toward the river. Upon reaching the crowded landing he heard news that sickened him. Hardly a mile away, the boat had struck a sawyer which tore a great hole in its hull, and had sunk.

His feet aching with the bruises which his thin mocassins could not prevent, he hurried along the bank. The stricken craft was in a perilous position. It rested on the river bottom, listing dangerously, while the crew, passengers and Indians worked furiously at salvaging what cargo they could. Father de Smet gave himself vigorously to the task. On board the boat were a season's food supplies for the mission, ornaments for the little church, a tabernacle, a bell, and clothes for himself and his colleagues.

When the work of saving all possible cargo had been completed, the people of the Council Bluffs faced a sad reckoning. The loss was estimated at more than $40,000. All provisions for the Indians had been swept away in the raging current. Of the goods consigned to the mission, only a few articles had been recovered: a plough, a saw, a pair of boots and some wine.

Bravely Father de Smet wrote to a friend in his native Belgium:

> Providence was still favorable to us. With the help of the plough, we were abled to plant a large field of corn; it was the season for furrowing. We are using the saw to build a better house and enlarge our church, already too small. With my boots I can walk in the woods and prairies without fear of being bitten by the serpents which throng there. And the wine permits us to offer to God every day the most holy sacrifice of the mass, a privilege that has been denied us during a long time.
>
> We therefore returned with courage and resignation to the acorns and roots.

The steamboat brought new kinds of men into the Indian country, kinds never before seen there and which had no rightful places in the scheme of things. Gamblers, thieves, swindlers, confidence men, murderers, escaped convicts, false prophets could ride the river boats, take their prey, and return to their hideouts before winter imprisoned them beyond the frontier.

"The country is overrun with vagabond Americans, with riffraff," Father de Smet reported, "and the Government, which alone could put a stop to this abominable traffic . . . pays no attention."

Traveling with unprecedented swiftness up the Missouri, the steamboat brought other scourges – venereal diseases, fevers, maladies never before known there and which the Indians had no means of fighting.

The *St. Peters* brought smallpox.

It was a tragedy that might easily have been averted. Officers of the American Fur Company, owners of the boat, were aboard when several cases of the disease were discovered. They had ample time to turn it back before reaching the upper river, but to have done that would have meant the loss of the summer's trade. They might have unloaded the cargo, fumigated it, and set it on up the river in keelboats, but to have done that would have meant an increase in the cost of operations.

They did neither. The *St. Peters,* carrying a cargo of death, went on. The company officers stupidly attempted to keep Indians from coming near it. If they had commanded the sun not to rise they would have known as much success. The Indians knew the boat carried supplies for them, and they suspected that the efforts to keep them away from it were part of a scheme to cheat them. They swarmed about it, and virtually everything they touched sealed their doom.

On the *St. Peters* went, spreading the deadly bane. Hundreds of Indians died each day. So many bodies were there that it was impossible for those not stricken to bury them, and they were thrown over cliffs and into gullies and into the river. For miles about most villages a terrible stench filled the air.

Of the twelve hundred members of the Mandans, only thirty persons escaped the contagion.

On each side of the river for five hundred miles, between Fort Pierre and the Yellowstone, Indian lodges stood but no smoke rose from them, no sounds of human life except the wails and screams of the dying broke the fearful silence. Brave warriors in countless numbers killed themselves, unable to stand the sight of flesh rotting on their women and children.

More than fifteen thousand Indians were the victims of the greed and coldness and criminal negligence of the men who worked for John Jacob Astor on the Missouri River. Astor criticized them not at all. He took no notice of the situation. Had they lost the season's trade as the result of a humane act, however, they would have heard his thunder and suffered from his wrath. Human lives were not to be compared in value to beaver skins. You could make no money being humane to Indians.

Obtaining sufficient wood for fuel was a constant and difficult problem.

Along the lower river wide groves ranged back from the banks, sometimes for miles, and there a new enterprise bolstered the sparse economy. Settlers from the mouth as far out as Westport established woodyards, but they were not dependable supply depots. For a year or two a man might augment his income with cutting and splitting trees into bolts suitable for the boilers – oak, cottonwood, chestnut, elm, maple, hickory, walnut – and then abandon the project. A steamboat captain could never depend upon securing wood in a certain place. He took it where he could find it, and if he could not find it, he was obliged to put a crew ashore to cut some.

The magnificent forests along the lower river made it possible for a captain to obtain wood somehow, either by buying it or cutting it, but this advantageous situation rapidly diminished. The rolling hills over which the great trees marched soon melted into ever-widening prairies. The woodlands broke apart into scattered islands, and at last only a few trees remained to trace the crooked courses of shallow streams across flat earth that touched the sky, the grass sea of the high plains growing steadily more immense, sweeping onward for a thousand miles until it washed against the towering impregnable wall of the western mountains.

Two sources of supply made it possible for a boat to make the journey through the great northern plains. One was the cottonwood tree. It needed comparatively little water, and in many areas it was the only tree which could survive. Along the streams in which some water always flowed, the cottonwood stood in stately groves, whispering with the slightest stirring of the airs. In the lands which knew searing drouths it lifted misshapen tortured limbs in supplication to a merciless sky. On the high plains, it appeared like a green thread marking the ways of seepage water.

The other source of supply on the upper river was, strangely enough, the river itself. Often in changing its course, the river would sweep away a cottonwood forest. The trees would be uprooted, and in the mire and swamplands they would be piled up into great white woodyards. On every trip upstream a captain would take note of the driftwood, but never could he be certain that he would find a supply where he had last seen it. Almost invariably the channel changed each year. He might take on driftwood in one place on an outbound voyage, and the next spring find that place several miles from the channel he was obliged to follow.

Captain Joseph A. Sire kept journals of many of his trips, writing in French, the language which almost everyone on the frontier, except the Americans from the Appalachian woodlands, understood. The distance from St. Louis to Fort Union varied over the years from 1760 to 1800 miles, depending upon changes in the Missouri's navigable course. Captain Sire recorded that his trip up the river in 1841 took eighty days, and the return journey twenty-one days. Improvements in machinery, more favorable weather, the good fortune to obtain wood when needed, and sufficient water in the river, made possible a steady decrease in the time consumed by the round trip during the next six years. In 1847, Captain Sire reported that the upstream voyage took only forty days, and he brought his boat back to St. Louis from Fort Union in fourteen days. Going out the average distance covered was forty-four miles. Returning an average distance of 123 miles was traveled.

The log of Captain Sire's boat, *Omega,* in 1843 provided a graphic illustration of the unceasing struggle to obtain wood for the boilers. On this voyage he had with him in the wheelhouse Joseph Le Barge, most famous of all Missouri River pilots and masters.

The 1843 log of the *Omega* covers sixty-five days between the departure from St. Louis in late April and the return in late June. In that period, Captain Sire made ninety-seven entries about wood which reveal the ordeal he faced in obtaining enough to keep his boat going.

The locations of trading posts were frequently changed. A company might erect a post on a site thought to be favorable for trade with Indians, but when the trade failed to materailize it would be abandoned. Perhaps changes in the ever-unpredictable river might force traders to move their post to safer ground. Tribal wars, robbery, disease, murder were other reasons why posts were left to stand forlorn and unoccupied.

Few remained in a deteriorating condition for any length of time. A steamboat soon put into the bank before an abandoned post, and axes and saws in the hands of the crew had soon leveled the stockade and the buildings. It was a prize every captain hoped to come upon, for the wood of a post usually was dry, could be easily cut, and produced good boiler fires. Moreover, it cost nothing but the effort to take it on board. Not a few owners who temporarily left their posts unoccupied returned to find them gone – cut up into cord wood by the crew of a passing steamboat.

It took only fifteen years for the furtraders to conquer the Missouri with the steamboat.

The new way of life, born with the arrival of the *Pike,*

brought greater wickedness than the West had ever known. Every advantage was counter-balanced by tragedy, horror and despair. Every benefit created soil in which greed, venality and immorality fluorished. Every new opportunity gave roots to new kinds of crime, violence and disease never before experienced or suffered.

Over every cross and altar the shadow of evil lay beside the light of progress.

1822

TURNING NUMBER FOUR

———◆———

Monopoly on the Missouri

The insuperable alliance of big business
and national political power
reaches the West

IV

Monopoly on the Missouri

I have tought a good Deal on the proposi-
tion made me Some time Since by your frinds
to make Some genral arrangement for the
Indian Trade & if our Government Do
exclude Canada traders from aur Cauntry
as I believe they will the trade will become
an object & I would Licke to cam to the
arrangement of which I will thank you
to Inform tham.
> John Jacob Astor to
> Charles Gratiot in St. Louis

That letter, written early in 1816, meant more than it said. It meant that, after nearly a decade of observation and contemplation, the world's most powerful fur trader had reached the decision to enter directly into the fur trade of St. Louis and the Missouri River.[1]

That was what Astor at last had made up his mind to do—extend the operations of the American Fur Company west of the Mississippi River—but if he saw himself moving *directly* toward that attainment, a different view of his actions might understandably have been held by others. That would have been a situation to his liking.

In Astor's way of thinking, the word *directly* did not necessarily indicate an advance in a straight line from a certain starting point to a specific goal. He had his goal,

---

[1] For additional reading on this period of Astor's career consult chapter II, footnote 1.

and he would move relentlessly toward it, but the twist-
ings and turnings which would mark his route would be
seen by him as nothing more than temporary deviations
made mandatory by circumstances. If a circular course
was not the shortest road to a destination, it did not mean
that it was not the most strategic and the most profitable.

He not only understood fully the value of deviousness,
but he was a master of it. Undue haste he considered
one of man's greatest weaknesses, and he took pride in
the knowledge that he had never been guilty of it. That
he did not propose to jeopardize this record in launching
his trans-Mississippi offensive, needed no demonstration
now. He had made that clear several times in the past
ten years, ever since the return of Lewis and Clark and
the first ascension of the Upper Missouri by American
fur traders. All this time he had been fully cognizant of
the potentialities of the immense new territory that had
been opened east of the mountains, yet he had stead-
fastly refrained from making any move that he had not
calculated to the best of his ability would be beneficial
to him.

The disaster he had suffered on the Columbia had
not been the result of his own rashness, not a reflection
on his intelligence or denoting a lack of perspicacity.
It had been the result of events he could not foresee –
indeed, no man could have foreseen them – and develop-
ments which he had no means of preventing. The loss
of Astoria had, however, served as a forcible illustration
of the wisdom of his feeling about St. Louis and the upper
Missouri country.

Before the War of 1812, Gratiot had been the one
St. Louis businessman who had publicly voiced the opin-

ion that it would be advantageous for all concerned if Astor could be counted as a friend and colleague in the Missouri River trade rather than an antagonist. The other traders had bluntly dismissed the thought, contrarily resolving to keep Astor out at all cost.

They could not stop him from buying furs in St. Louis, or from selling merchandise to St. Louis houses – actually, the majority of them understood from personal experience that doing business with him in these two respects proffered certain benefits – but they could, if they stood together, prevent him from acquiring stock in St. Louis companies. As they were to learn to their sorrow, this attitude represented an exaggerated idea of their own powers and capabilities. If every house engaged in the Missouri River trade had been merged into a single company, its resources would have been insignificant in comparison to those of Astor. As for capabilities, no amalgamation of these assets would have equaled those Astor alone possessed.

Reorganization of the Missouri Fur Company was made necessary by the expiration of the original agreement which had created it, and in November 1811, Gratiot wrote Astor about the matter. It was his thought that Astor might wish to participate in financing the new company, which would have a capital investment of $50,000. Shares cost $3,000, and Gratiot thought it might be possible for Astor to obtain five of them. He revealed his shrewdness with the suggestion that such an investment would be favorable to Astor's desire to "draw the furr trade into your hands."

Gratiot's counsel and proposals fell on deaf ears – those of his associates and of Astor. The partners were determined not to let Astor get a foot in their door.

However, Astor had no intention of making the effort. He saw serious weaknesses in the structure of the new company. Almost every trader of standing in St. Louis was a partner, and all of them were allowed to participate in the administration of its affairs. Astor wanted no part of an organization that did not have a single capable individual in control of its management.

He replied to Gratiot:

"I Do Not knaw that I would be interested even if the company wished it, if hawever I can by any means be of use to tham I shall be happey in So Doing."

His offer to be of "use" was not a polite gesture nor did it come from the goodness of his heart. In Astor's character, politeness and goodness were weapons he used at propitous moments, not simply admirable qualities. He was fully aware that war with England — and it appeared inevitable — would create havoc in the Missouri trade. The flow of trade goods from Canada would be dammed at the ports of entry. Exportation of American furs to Montreal would be prohibited. These circumstances would place him in a very advantageous position to be of "use" to the St. Louis companies.

He was, of course, right. That was what happened. The structure of the Missouri Fur Company began to weaken. When at last the conflict ended, there were half a dozen small houses struggling to survive, none of them large enough to overcome competition, and all of them too insecure financially to undertake dangerous expeditions far up the river. As he closely observed the conditions, Astor kept Gratiot busy buying furs for him. He bought every pelt available, mostly deerskins, as there were few other kinds coming into St. Louis.

In 1816, he deemed the time had come to take another major step in his invasion of the Missouri.

John P. Cabanne, an enterprising merchant-trader, had obtained a quantity of merchandise from Astor during the war. When peace came, Cabanne proposed that Astor decline to sell goods to any other St. Louis house. Under such an arrangement, Cabanne pointed out, he would be in a position to buy large quantities of trade goods from Astor and profitably distribute it.

Astor had good reason to laugh to himself as he rejected the proposition. In 1816, European goods suitable for the western Indian trade, stopped from coming into the United States for nearly four years, would continue to be in short supply for at least another twelve to fourteen months. Astor's stocks, as a result of wartime smuggling and heavy prewar buying, were the largest in the country. Cabanne would, indeed, have an advantage if he were the only Astor outlet in St. Louis.

Astor saw no reason not to retain that advantage for himself, and he did. He ordered Robert Stuart and Ramsay Crooks to move into St. Louis with a sizeable supply of goods, in this quiet way making it appear that he was setting out to establish his own traders in the Missouri River Indian trade without further delay. That was not his intention—not yet.

In refusing Cabanne's offer, however, he wrote him that he had supplied Stuart and Crooks with goods "for the purpose of trading with Indians &c in your quater of the Cauntry. Sorry to say that I am under Several Engagements . . . which must be complyd with on my part. . . I will make no more which can possibly tend to Injure any of my friends."

This was unadulterated hokum. Astor had no friends in St. Louis with whom he had trade agreements. Stuart and Crooks were his chief lieutenants, but even their friendship for him was suspect. Their actions were affected little, if at all, by sentiment. They were interested in making money, and participation in Astor's program as they understood it proffered that opportunity.

Next Astor wrote to Gratiot suggesting that he persuade Cabanne to take over the goods furnished Stuart and Crooks and give them "Some Compensation for time Lost."

The seemingly complicated and confused methods Astor invariably employed in approaching a paramount objective were never better illustrated than in this instance. Stuart and Crooks had not even reached St. Louis when he proposed that they dispose of their goods, not in the Indian trade, but to Cabanne. Obviously he was using Gratiot, to pave the way for negotiations he had secretly instructed Stuart and Crooks to carry out. Gratiot, the trustworthy and highly respected trader who had sought to open doors for Astor when all of them were tightly shut and barred against him, at once conferred with not only Cabanne but others.

When Stuart and Crooks did arrive, in the summer of 1816, Gratiot had succeeded in removing many of the obstacles that might have stood as serious impediments to the success of their true mission. They were able to fashion agreements with Cabanne and Company and with the house of Berthold and Chouteau. Both companies were bound to trade exclusively with Astor, and in return they had Astor's promise not to send his own outfits to trade on the Missouri as long as the contracts endured.

Perhaps Gratiot was smarter than Cabanne, Berthold and Chouteau, for he wrote Astor: ".   .   .   it appears to me that all rivalls for the Indian Trade will soon be over, & fore see a disposition in all those who are concerned to come together to Some understanding."

In reality, Astor's promise to keep out of the Missouri River trade while the agreements were in force had little value, for it was implicit in the agreements that they would be reopened and revised as the parties deemed necessary each spring. Actually, Astor had agreed to keep from entering directly into the Indian trade on the Missouri for no longer than one year. He could not be forced to sign a new contract containing provisions he did not consider advantageous to him.

Gratiot had received a commission of two per cent of the value of the furs he had secured for Astor during the war years. He badly needed more income now, for his own affairs had steadily deteriorated to the point that he was in serious financial difficulties. He wrote Astor asking for orders to make more purchases.

"I have made Some arrangements with aur frinds in your plaise," Astor coldly informed him, "and as they seem to be excallent men I wish to please them. . . it is on this account that I Do not now Give you an order for Skins."

Gratiot had been the only man in St. Louis who had made any effort at all to be a friend to Astor. With those few words, Astor kicked him out of the way. Before another year had passed Gratiot was dead.

Astor continued to give the appearance that he held only a casual interest in events taking place in St. Louis, but the pose was completely deceptive. He was in reality keeping a close watch on them, while he sent his brigades smashing through the region of the Great Lakes on his drive to dominate all the fur trade between Niagara and the St. Peters, between Michilimackinac and the Ohio.

If the St. Louis traders were mystified by Astor's slowness or reticence to cross the Mississippi with similar forces, they were not unaware of what was happening in the vast territory to the east and north of them, the territory which Astor called the Northern Department of the American Fur Company. They were seeing a full-scale demonstration of his incomparable power. Being thankful that he had as yet given no indication that an invasion of their territories was imminent had little therapeutic effect upon the concern which continued to grow in them as they watched his juggernaut, spewing its corruption and debauchery, its bribery and destruction, its terrorism and brutality, roll across Michigan, Wisconsin, Illinois, Indiana, Ohio and the valley of the upper Mississippi, crushing all in its path. They could see the shadow of the irresistible machine, a shadow that came steadily closer as they watched.

The Missouri River trade was recovering from the devastating effects of the war. Lisa had big plans. He had taken over Cabanne and Company, found it a poor prospect and had liquidated it. This eliminated one of the houses with which Astor had agreements, but Lisa's action had not been taken with the hope of injuring Astor. He formed a new association, and applied to Crooks for goods with the intention of sending an expedition to the upper river.

This had the effect of forcing Astor's hand, and it

was soon apparent that his policy of supplying St. Louis companies had been revised. Crooks refused to furnish Lisa with goods, declaring they were not available. Lisa knew better. He promptly began to inject new life into the doddering Missouri Fur Company, a move thoughtfully observed by Astor and Crooks.

Lisa was able to enlist new money and new partners, among them a number of able and experienced traders, such as Thomas Hempstead, Joshua Pilcher, Joseph Perkins, Andrew Woods, Moses Carson, John B. Zenoni, Andrew Drips and Robert Jones.

Astor's contract with Berthold and Chouteau was still in effect, but Chouteau, undoubtedly envisioning adversities ahead, announced he would like to buy some shares in the American Fur Company. Astor, fully cognizant of Chouteau's capabilities as a businessman and trader, not to mention his high position as a member of the leading and most influential family in St. Louis, was not averse to some financial arrangement with him. Berthold, who thoroughly despised Astor even though he was willing to do business with him, opposed the idea. Crooks, whom Astor had instructed to conduct negotiations with Berthold and Chouteau, became aggravated by repeated delays. "Perhaps," he wrote Astor, "the appearance of David Stone and Company (Stone, Bostwick & Company) at St. Louis may rouse them from their fancied security and turn their attention seriously this way."

This statement indicated that Astor definitely wanted some type of financial agreement with Berthold and Chouteau. Later events demonstrated that he had in mind absorbing them by making them partners with small holdings. In any case, Crook's prediction that the advent of Stone, Bostwick and Company would have an effect on the situation was sound.

Stone had been driven from the Great Lakes region by Astor after a long and strenuous battle. He had moved into the Missouri River trade with rapidity and an alarming display of energy. On Stone's heels had come a strong group of Boston traders. Their expeditions began to drive into territories in which the older houses had long enjoyed dominant positions. Following the sudden death of Lisa, Joshua Pilcher, a man of great ability, became head of the Missouri Fur Company. Within a short time he had sent more than three hundred men up the Missouri.

Suddenly another new and strong competitor appeared. The Columbia Fur Company had been founded by Joseph Renville, a Canadian who had been made footlose by the amalgamation of the Hudson's Bay and the North West companies. He had been joined by other traders, most of them wilderness veterans, who also had been injured by the merger, among them Kenneth McKenzie, William Laidlaw, Honore Picott and James Kipp. Although they did not have a large capital, they presented a formidable front. They not only plunged into the Missouri River trade but launched a fierce opposition against Astor in the Upper Mississippi and Wisconsin areas, establishing posts as far east as Green Bay. To circumvent the federal law which forbade foreigners from engaging in the fur trade in the United States they took into partnership two Americans, Daniel Lamont and a little known trader named Tilton, and they registered the name of their organization as Tilton & Company.

It was clear that with so many companies in the field a dog-eat-dog condition would soon develop, to the detriment of all – all, that is, unless someone was able to step into the conflict and by effecting consolidations through purchases achieve an advantageous position.

That "someone" could have been no one but Astor, for no one else possessed the required experience and resources to carry out such a program.

Astor gave Crooks orders.

Berthold and Chouteau received an ultimatum: sell out to Astor and work for him, or take the consequences. When they continued to hesitate, Astor ordered Crooks to proceed in establishing a Western Department of the American Fur Company.

Astor recognized that open warfare with the Columbia Fur Company would be costly and time-consuming. His next command to Crooks was to open negotiations for either an outright purchase or a consolidation.

Samuel Abbott, manager of the important American Fur Company post at Prairie du Chien, was transferred to St. Louis to take charge of the office, warehouse and trading store Crooks opened there in the spring of 1822.

Astor had driven Stone out of Mackinac and Detroit. Now he approached him not as an enemy but in a spirit of friendship. He offered to appoint Stone his chief St. Louis agent. The terms were reasonable, and Stone, glancing backward for a moment, understood the folly of resistance. A consolidation was completed. It included the Stone affiliate, Munson & Barnard, and was to run three and a half years, from April 21, 1823, to October 1, 1826.

The Astor juggernaut had crossed the Mississippi.

That it had not intimidated all traders, however, was quickly demonstrated by General William H. Ashley, who launched the first of the series of expeditions that would make him both rich and famous. Because Ashley's ventures and the revolutionary ideas he executed marked a vital turning in the course of western history, they will be considered in a separate section of this work.

Astor thoughtfully studied the moves and plans of the energetic General. Meanwhile, he settled upon a policy which eventually would dominate the strategy of his opposition, not only of Ashley but of the menacing Columbia Fur Company, the revived Missouri Fur Company, and other challengers.

The policy was not new, but it was reconstructed and bolstered to meet the peculiar demands and exigencies of the moment. Fundamentally it presented the thoroughness, methodicalness, caution and patience which had so successfully served him in conquering the trade of the Great Lakes region. He saw no reason why it should not be equally advantageous in the West.

Astor was in no sense a pioneer. He had no desire to be an explorer or a discoverer, for he saw no profit in suffering the hardships which were unavoidable in such fields. He had not sent his expeditions to the Columbia to find out what was there. He knew what was there, he knew the fortunes in furs that awaited the taking there, for his ships had traded along the north Pacific coast and with the Russians in Alaska. The Canadians had opened the Great Lakes country long before he had bought his first muskrat skin on the New York docks. The Mountain Men had opened the American West long before he had sent Crooks to St. Louis to establish a Western Department.

Astor was a gambler, but not of the card-playing kind. He was a gambler only in the sense that all financiers must take some chances, simply because certain hazards are inherent in every investment of dollars. They cannot be avoided, but they can be reduced to a relatively safe minimum.

Crooks's thinking followed a similar pattern. They were in complete accord with the view that plunging into the Missouri River trade without restraint, in a full-scale open offensive, would be unwise, dangerous and excessively expensive. Let the Pilchers and the Ashleys and the McKenzies and others do the hard work of building posts and establishing the trade on the upper Missouri and out in the mountains, let them suffer the losses of men, merchandise and furs which must surely come with the initiation of new trading projects among the western tribes. The Blackfeet were a case in point. No one had succeeded in making peace with them. Their furs still went to the Canadian posts. All the Americans had got for their efforts in the Blackfoot country had been a disastrous loss of goods and lives. The result of any further efforts undoubtedly would be the same.

Astor watched and waited, and he saw that the men of the Missouri and Columbia Fur companies were wise in the selection of sites for their posts. Each stood at or near a confluence of rivers, the natural centers of trade, reachable over courses of least resistance, and accessible from several directions. When he built, Astor told Crooks, he would go to these same places. The system would be the same as that employed in the Northern

Department. They would go in and buy out the others, absorb them, or destroy them. The weapons would be the same as those used in the Great Lakes country — lower prices, superior merchandise, credit, minimum expenses and alcohol, unlimited quantities of alcohol — invade, undersell and destroy.

Crooks dispatched a dozen outfits up the river on seasonal journeys during the first two years after he opened the Western Department, but he built only three posts. One stood on the left bank of the Missouri between the present cities of St. Joseph and Omaha. Another was just above the mouth of the Platte. The other was on the right bank just beyond White River, and near it were the Columbia Fur Company's post, Fort Lookout, and the Missouri Fur Company's post, Fort Recovery.

Progress of the Western Department was aggravatingly slow, but it began to look as if the plan to let others do the perilous work of opening doors would continue to pay dividends.

On his first expedition up the river, General Ashley had lost a keelboat carrying a cargo valued at more than $10,000. On his second expedition the following year his company had been attacked at the Arikara Villages and turned back. Thirteen trappers had been killed and nearly as many were wounded.

Jones and Immel of the Missouri Fur Company and five of their trappers were killed by Blackfeet. Four others were wounded but escaped. All the property of the expedition, horses, traps, goods and furs, valued at $15,000, had been stolen.

It would be generous to suggest that Astor felt sorry for the men who had lost their lives, but merely logical to believe that his feeling about the financial losses was one of satisfaction.

Yet, his sanguineness was somewhat shaken by another situation in the far upper river territory. On several occasions the British had been successful in inducing Indians to attack American trappers. A number had been slain and their furs taken, unquestionably delivered into the hands of British traders. Not a cent of Astor money had been lost in these tragic incidents, but he could understand that the continued existence of such a condition presented a potential menace to his own interests. After all, the time would come – and perhaps not too far in the future – when his own men would be in the area in which the British were perpetrating their savage acts. He sent his emissaries in Washington to thunder in the State and War departments against such outrages – foreign saboteurs and plunderers fomenting attacks on Americans engaged in honest pursuits on American soil.

Washington would get around to registering diplomatic protests against the British invaders, but it could do nothing about chastizing the Blackfeet. The best solution of that problem, at least for the present, would be for trappers to keep out of Blackfeet territory.

Ashley appeared to be in a position to carry on, but the Missouri Fur Company clearly was staggering from the blow inflcted by the loss of the Jones and Immel expedition. It restricted its operations to the lower Missouri and the Platte. Pilcher was a thoroughly discouraged man. Astor concluded that he would need no forceful assault to complete its demise. It would fall of its own accord, and he could afford to wait.

He understood, however, that too much patience could be as unfruitful as ill-timed action, and now he began to fear that Crooks had been guilty of making such an error. He could cite several obvious opportunities of which Crooks had failed to take advantage. Purchases of furs by the Western Department had been generally too small and less profitable than they should have been. Numerous houses, even some of the smallest, had enjoyed transactions in which he might well have participated. A previously little known firm, Bernard Pratte & Company, was becoming increasingly successful. In 1825, it and Columbia had obtained control of nearly all the buffalo hides and beaver skins brought into St. Louis, a feat nothing less than intolerable and which had made Astor's blood pressure mount.

Stone, Bostwick and Company was not living up to expectations, and Astor expressed a desire to be rid of them.

Perhaps Crooks had been giving too much attention to another and more romantic consideration, an attractive young lady named Miss Emelie Pratte. The Pratte family was hardly less prominent than the Chouteaus, and they were related to them by blood ties.

Astor was not so ungallant as to suggest that Crook's marriage to Miss Emelie had been influenced by such considerations, but he readily admitted that it was not a misfortune for either the groom or him. Crooks had become a member of the old and distinguished (and rich) Chouteau-Pratte clan. He couldn't have done better in St. Louis.

Astor saw the necessity of putting the spurs to Crooks. First, however, he wanted his own plans fully developed, he wanted to be sure of where he was going, before he issued orders to proceed. Stone, Bostwick and Company had to be eliminated, and he analyzed the structure, financial strength and personnel of every St. Louis house in a search for a successor. Most of the companies were quickly dismissed as unsuitable.

Crooks had signed an agreement with Menard & Valle, a small concern operating chiefly on the Illinois and Mississippi rivers. Under the contract, Menard & Valle would buy all goods from Astor, and Astor would have the first refusal of their furs. For a brief time Astor considered building up Menard & Valle as major agents, then decided against the idea. After all, they were already in the fold.

He was well aware that the time would come when he must attack General Ashley, but that time was not the year of 1826. The bulk of Ashley's trade was conducted in the mountains, and he concluded it would be unwise to invade that remote field until his affairs on the river were firmly organized and more favorable to him.

The most desirable target was Columbia. Two years after its organization, Columbia and its subsidiary, Collier & Powell, which operated chiefly in the upper Mississippi and northern Wisconsin areas, had been more than $50,000 in debt. This was due almost entirely to Astor's opposition in the Northern Department. He would have licked them there in time, and have driven them out, but Columbia had rapidly extended its operations westward to the upper Missouri. Its trade for a single season in that region had enabled it not only to liquidate all its debts but to make each partner a good profit. Since that time, while it continued to make little or no money in the Northern Department, its successes increased in the West.

Although he saw an urgent need to strengthen his position, Astor was not convinced he could accomplish it by a direct assault on Columbia. That would consume too much time, as well as require needless expenditures. He concluded that the same results could be achieved with a flank approach, the method he had used so successfully in the past. He would strike where he was least expected.

Astor's shrewdness was never better demonstrated than when he selected Bernard Pratte and Company as his first victim. Destruction of that organization, however, was not in the plan he formulated. On the contrary, he would eliminate the unsatisfactory Stone, Bostwick by purchasing it, and then make Bernard Pratte the leading agents dealing with the Western Department.

In this strategy, social as well as financial rank was given due consideration. One of the chief partners of Bernard Pratte was Pierre Chouteau, Junior.

Chouteau had suspected the trend of Astor's scheming before it became generally known. Possibly he was alerted by the newest member of the Pratte family, Ramsay Crooks. In any case, he wasted no time in attempting to arrange an agreement with the Columbia Fur Company for a joint effort in the mountains in the coming year. "It becomes necessary," he wrote Kenneth McKenzie, Columbia's president, "to learn from you with the least possible loss of time what is to be done to prosecute the business in the Rocky Mountains, which is intended to be carried on through the medium of your Upper Missouri Outfit."

It was quick thinking on Chouteau's part. His company had much to gain by securing an alliance with Columbia before Astor knocked on their door with a cheque in hand. However, Astor was moving too fast now to permit that to happen.

Chouteau, who would become a wealthy railroad and industrial magnate, had wanted for years to buy shares in the American Fur Company, but had been dissuaded by his associates. Now he argued that it would be sheer folly for them not to come to some accord with Astor. In fact, he saw it as extremely good fortune that they had a chance to become affiliated with the most powerful corporation of its kind in the United States, and he warned that once Astor had started his insuperable machine rolling up the Missouri Valley they, like all others, would be crushed by it. Astor wanted them. That was all to their advantage, for it meant that Astor would make concessions.

Chouteau's partners gave up any thought of attempting to oppose Astor. A four-year agreement with him was quickly signed, one highly favorable to Bernard Pratte and Company. It and the Western Department would share equally the profits (or losses) of the trade conducted on the Missouri and its tributaries, and in the Mississippi country below Prairie du Chien. Astor would have first opportunity of taking all furs collected, and he would receive a commission on all sales. In return he would advance the money needed for all operations, and there were unmistakable indications that these would be of considerable size.

Stone capitulated without a struggle. He had learned

long before the futility of fighting Astor. The affairs of his company were in bad shape, and Astor was obliged to assume several debts for which he was not responsible in order to terminate the purchase. He grumbled, and dismissed the matter. Far more important burdens weighed on him, and his eyes were gazing far up the Missouri.

Crooks had responded to the prod, and he was busily engaged in organizing expeditions to open a number of small posts on the Riviere au Jacques, one at the Forks of the Cheyenne, and another at the confluence of the Cheyenne and the Missouri. They would set out early in the spring of 1827, as soon as the river was free of ice.

The agreement with Bernard Pratte had become operative in January. Prices for furs were strong in New York, but were depressed in Europe. Astor's superb commercial instincts, however, indicated to him that a general rise was in the offing. While he publicly displayed a pessimistic attitude, he began to make exceptionally heavy purchases. The year 1827 was not a third gone before he held corners on beaver, buffalo, muskrat, bear and otter. His position in the New York market was worth no less than a million dollars net profit to him.

"You will be surprised," he wrote Crooks as he began to reap the harvest, "to learn the quantity of Muskrats I sold in less than 24 hours .   .   .   altogether 550,000 .   .   .   so many in the world have never been sold in one day. . . the average price is about 36 cents   .   . ."

Crooks was frantically attempting to buy furs in St. Louis on Astor's account, but he was meeting with serious difficulties. He offered to take all the muskrats and buffalo Columbia could deliver, but McKenzie raised the price beyond all reason. Things had gone smoothly in transactions with Bernard Pratte for several months, but now Crooks found himself facing roadblocks placed in his path by his own relatives.

The agreement with Bernard Pratte provided that Astor was to be given the first opportunity to purchase furs the firm had bought from trappers and other traders. It did not provide that Bernard Pratte had to sell to Astor if it considered Astor's offering prices too low.

Pratte and Chouteau had no intention of helping Astor to corner the St. Louis market without substantial profits to themselves.

The truth was that Columbia and Collier & Powell owned half the buffalo robes that were for sale, and they had large inventories of beaver, otter and other furs. Bernard Pratte owned the other half of the available buffalo hides, and they also had large quantities of otter and beaver. Astor would have no chance of getting control without these stocks, and no one understood that better than McKenzie, Pratte and Chouteau.

Astor's wrath had no more effect on them than did his pleas. When he continued his refusal to pay the prices they asked, Pratte himself went into the New York market and sold large quantities of beaver and otter under Astor's nose.

Astor publicly charged that Pratte had sold the skins for the same price he had offered. This was not the truth. Pratte had sold his beaver at $5 to $5.12½ a pound. Astor's highest offer was $4 to $4.12½.

His failure to acquire Pratte's beaver, Astor told

Crooks, had prevented him from keeping prices up in New York, for "Had I gotten it I would have sent it out of the country to China. . . he has forfeited everything with me. . . Had Mr. Pratte acted candidly with me, it would have been greatly to our mutual benefit. I am sorry to say I lost all confidence in him."

This was something less than an honest statement. Astor's anger stemmed entirely from the fact that he had been denied an extra profit of a dollar a pound. He understood that Pratte had acted entirely within his own right. Astor's protest of disloyalty was nothing more than a smoke-screen hiding his own chagrin. Moreover, he was aware that the episode was an irrefutable demonstration of his sound judgment in selecting agents. Pratte and Chouteau were shrewd and determined men, not to be intimidated by anyone. He had lost nothing more than a skirmish, and his association with them would, in the end, pay large dividends. Of that he felt certain. At least he had nearly four more years to prove himself right or wrong.

The case of the Columbia Fur Company was another matter. He knew now that he could let no more time pass without facing it squarely in a showdown fight. The bars were down, he told Crooks, but still warned against advancing in a frontal attack.

The specific orders Crooks received were to feel out Columbia regarding a division of operations in the Northern Department. Crooks was to begin by suggesting that exclusive trade areas might be established for both the American Fur Company and Columbia, to their mutual benefit.

Crooks opened a cautious correspondence with Mc-
Kenzie and Daniel Lamont, another Columbia partner.
The letters revealed that they were willing to discuss
such a plan, but did not reveal their strong suspicions.
When Astor indicated a willingness to give up territory
to a competitor, that was reason enough to conclude
that the least of his motives was a sincere desire for
peace. Striving to discern Astor's strategy, McKenzie
tentatively suggested St. Croix as a dividing line. That
would have involved the abandonment by Astor of the
valuable St. Peters region from Traverse des Sioux
upward.

Astor promptly rejected the proposal as wholly un-
acceptable, but he instructed Crooks to keep the door
open by proposing a conference at Prairie du Chien or
Fort Snelling. Now it was learned that McKenzie's contract with the other eight partners of Columbia would
expire late in 1827, and Crooks, was ordered to approach
him about entering the service of the American Fur
Company.

Crooks did, but he did not like the idea, and he wrote
Astor: "To secure even Mr. McKenzie would be very
desirable for he is certainly the soul of his concern;
but I would prefer taking with him such of his partners
as are efficient traders, and might continue to annoy us
.   .   ."

Moreover, Crooks warned Astor, McKenzie was not
the kind of man who would desert his partners and
leave them to struggle with a weakened and disorganized
company. He was wrong about that. If McKenzie had
any such scruples, they were not revealed in written
or spoken word. He was right, however, in his opinion

that securing the services of McKenzie alone would not solve the problem, and might well complicate it. Pratte and Chouteau supported this view.

McKenzie's demands for himself were beyond all reason. Astor's reply was: *All negotiations are concluded.* In other words, let there be war, war more vicious than Columbia had ever known. He sent a dispatch to Stuart, in command in the Northern Department, ordering him to launch immediate attacks "above the falls of St. Anthony . . . not suffer them to triumph on the River of St. Peters. . . we must now fight harder than ever." Astor was not talking about trading maneuvers alone, such things as underselling, pouring more rotgut whiskey down the throats of Indians, or making them gifts. He was talking about violence, shooting, stealing, beating, killing.

Columbia, accepting the challenge, sought to strengthen itself by increasing its western operations. The partners were agreed that it was only a question of a short time before they would be forced to abandon their positions in the Upper Mississippi country. Not only Astor's resources but his armed forces would make that position untenable.

McKenzie sent Tilton and Kipp to build a new post among the Mandans. Other posts were established on the Big Knife, in the Assiniboine country, at Teton River, on the Riviere au Jacques, the Niobrara, the White, the Vermilion, the Big Sioux. Defiantly it opened an office in St. Louis to facilitate the purchasing of goods, and it shipped its furs by steamboat down the Mississippi to deep water vessels at New Orleans. It met with success among Indians along the international border who had for decades traded only with the British, and it began a profitable trade with the Crows under the afternoon shadows of the mountains – all moves demonstrating the great ability of its men.

Build a post beside every Columbia post on the Missouri, Astor told Crooks. Heavily armed companies began to move up the Missouri to carry out the order.

Now the firm of Menard & Valle, whose enterprise had never emerged from an overhanging shadow of lethargy, began to kick over the traces. It sold skins in New York without first offering them to Astor, and ordered trade goods from New York houses in violation of their agreement. Punitive actions were required, and Astor did not let his occupation with the big war with Columbia deter him from inflicting them.

Without warning Western Department traders invaded the territory of Menard & Valle. They paid high prices for furs, and they sold goods at prices far below those any firm could meet and remain in business. In three months, Menard & Valle closed their doors.

Perhaps the ruthlessness and swiftness with which Astor destroyed this small house influenced McKenzie's thinking to some extent, but most likely the change of mind he underwent was brought about by the sight of the great Astor brigades moving up the river, hundreds of men armed not only with powder and shot, but with keelboats low in the water with trade goods and barrels of alcohol that would be sacrificed without profit if necessary. McKenzie let it be known that he was willing to resume talks, if Astor wished.

Crooks didn't believe it, but he dutifully responded, and when he arrived on McKenzie's door step he was

astonished to be invited into the parlor. McKenzie dumb-
founded him, however, with the frank admission that his
high demands had been nothing more than bluff. Mc-
Kenzie had wanted more time to build up the resources
of his company by expanding its operations so that Astor
would have to pay a greater price for it. He had simply
been attempting to see how much he could squeeze out
of Astor, and he had found out. He had got war, war
that he did not want, for no company could make money
fighting an extended conflict with Astor. He and his
partners had known all along that evenutally they would
have to capitulate. Now they were ready. They would
entertain a new offer, if Astor cared to make one.

Astor did, and it was fairer than anyone might have
expected it to be. Astor had his reasons for that. He
wanted McKenzie and the other Columbia partners to
work for him, and he wanted them to come into the
American Fur Company on terms satisfactory to them.
A dissatisfied trader would be of no value to him.

The Columbia partners considered Astor's terms emi-
nently fair. They signed contracts which not only ten-
dered him their company, its real property, its furs, equipment and trade goods, but their own services. Their
books showed that the company's annual profits exceeded
$300,000.

On July 6, 1827, five years after he had established
his Western Department, Astor was in virtual control of
the Missouri River fur trade.

With the acquisition of Columbia, Astor got title to
seven major posts between the Council Bluffs and the
Mandan Villages, and a dozen smaller stations in the

upper Missouri Valley. Even more important, he acquired a tight, efficient and energetic organization of veteran clerks, trappers and *voyageurs*. He gave orders at once that it was to be disrupted as little as possible. Not even the name on the banner under which they had operated was to be changed. It would still be called the Upper Missouri Outfit, Columbia's name for it, all the valley above the Big Sioux River would be its sphere of operations, there would be no limit set on expansion, and Kenneth McKenzie would be in supreme command, subject only to orders from Crooks and himself.

Now the sign, AMERICAN FUR COMPANY—WESTERN DEPARTMENT, hung above the doors of twenty-two permanent and strategically located trading posts on the Upper Missouri system. Two score subsidiary or temporary posts fed their furs into these main stations. Competition was all but non-existent. What remained was inconsequential, like a terrier yapping at a bear. If the bear tired of the noise, a swipe of a paw would end it. When hunters, trappers, clerks and *voyageurs* spoke of the *company,* they meant only one. The word *opposition* was italicized by a smile.

When Astor conquered the region of the Great Lakes, the old Northwest Territories, he became the largest and most powerful fur trader in the world. Nothing more could be said of him in that respect after he had conquired the Missouri River. If he was bigger, the world was still the same size.

It could be said of him, however, that his resources in the western wilderness—his property, his money and his powers in all that vast territory between the mouth of the Missouri and the Canadian border, the headwaters of the Mississippi and the Yellowstone – were far greater than those of the United States government.

The American Fur Company was the first of the business giants to reach the American West. If it was not as big as many others which, thriving on richer fare of land, transportation and utilities, followed it in the next few decades, it was without a peer under the western sun for the twenty-five years of its life. Between any sunrise and sunset it brought to the financial wizard, the incomparable trader, the commercial genius who created it in 1808 and killed it in 1833, more money than all but a very few Americans made in a year – something in excess of a million dollars every twelve months, $2,736 a day, $114 an hour, day or night.

Yet, it was not enough to satisfy him. Almost without drawing a breath after his victory over Columbia, he requested the latest reports on the activities and plans of the intrepid men who had bought out General Ashley – Jedediah S. Smith, David E. Jackson and William L. Sublette. There would be no resting on laurels.

Crooks and Chouteau went to work to formulate strategy for the new conquest they knew would come. Astor waited with impatience to review it as he battled to save his failing health in his luxurious and beloved country house overlooking the Hell Gate. His eyes were reaching far beyond the garden walls, far out across the plains to greater walls, the Shining Mountains.

1824

TURNING NUMBER FIVE

Rendezvous in the Mountains

Introduction of new systems of supply
and transport drastically change
the far western fur trade

V

Rendezvous in the Mountains

TO

Enterprising Young Men.

THE subscriber wishes to engage ONE HUN-
DRED MEN, to ascend the river Missouri
to its source, there to be employed for one, two
or three years – For particulars enquire of Major Andrew Henry, near the Lead Mines, in the
County of Washington, (who will ascend with,
and command the party) or to the subscriber at
St. Louis.

February 13   *Wm. H. Ashley*

That advertisement, the most historically significant
ever printed in a newspaper west of the Mississippi River,
appeared in the *Missouri Gazette & Public Advertiser* on
February 13, 1822.

It was a spotlight on the threshold of an unparalleled
period in the American West. It was the birth certificate
of a new system of economics that wrought drastic transitions in trade and transport in the mountain wilderness.
It was a trumpet that called into assembly the most
illustrious, intrepid and capable Mountain Men who ever
trod western trails. It was the *letters patent* opening
gateways through which they passed to incomparable
conquests, supreme discoveries and undying glory.

If these things were true, however – and they unquestionably were – a word of clarification seems desirable.

The importance and real meaning of events may be understood only by seeing them in their true relationship to others.

Numerous historians of the West, and especially those who devote themselves specifically to the fur trade, refer to the years 1822 to 1830 as "the Ashley era." It is a convenient but hardly proper designation. Notable as the achievements of Ashley and his men were, as radically different as were the practices they introduced and pursued, all other men did not stand still or remain silent while they were being performed. All other occurrences of the time may not justifiably be relegated to the shadow of inconsequentiality.

These were the years, for example, in which Astor won his relentless campaign to monopolize the trade of the Missouri River. They were the years when fur production soared to records that were never to be surpassed. They were the years when the trade reached the zenith of its influence, not only as a dominant force in western commerce but in political, social and military trends and decisions.

In every respect, they were the "finest years," the "greatest years," of the fur trade of the American West.

That distinction rests indubitably in a large part, if not predominantly, on the feats of Ashley and his men. Yet, prior to 1822, neither Ashley nor the majority of the recruits who responded to his advertisement had been engaged to any extent in the fur trade. Ashley himself came suddenly upon the stage in that year, rose to stardom almost overnight, and as abruptly retired to a supporting role. Many of the traders and trappers who served ably and loyally under him met violent deaths.

Most of those who lived to continue after he had with-drawn remained unacclaimed, while a few achieved far greater fame than he, but, without exception, whether extraordinary or undistinguished, each secured for him-self a permanent station in the record of wilderness ad-venture.[1]

The designation *businessman and politician* is more appropriate in a description of Ashley than *fur trader,* although it was in the fur trade that he obtained his wealth. The statement in no way suggests that he was a man whose career was adversely affected by conflicting interests or a dual personality. Quite to the contrary, his commercial acumen, his profound knowledge of west-

---

[1] The most comprehensive, thorough and definitive work on Ashley, his lieutenants, and the period of their association in the fur trade is Dale L. Morgan, *The West of William H. Ashley,* Denver, 1964. See also Morgan's *Jedediah Smith,* Indianapolis, 1953; John E. Sunder, *Bill Sublette,* Norman, Okla., 1959; Harrison C. Dale, *The Ashley-Smith Explorations and Dis-covery of a Central Route to the Pacific,* Cleveland, 1918; J. Cecil Alter, *James Bridger,* Salt Lake City, 1925, and reprints; Don Berry, *A Majority of Scoundrels,* New York, 1961; Robert Campbell, "Correspondence, 1834-45," in *Glimpses of the Past,* St. Louis, Mo. Hist. Soc., 1941; Charles L. Camp, *James Clyman, Frontiersman,* San Francisco, 1928, and Portland, 1960; Joshua Pilcher, "Report on the Fur Trade," in *Sen. Exec. Doc. no. 90,* 22 Cong., 1 sess., Washington, 1832; Julia Altrocchi, *The Old California Trail,* Caldwell, Id., 1945; T. D. Bonner, *Life and Adventures of James P. Beckwourth,* New York, 1856; S. N. Carvalho, *Incidents of Travel and Adventure in the Far West,* New York, 1850; Stanley Vestal, *James Brid-ger: Mountain Man, New York,* 1946; Vincent Geiger and Wakeman Bry-arly, *The Trail to California,* New Haven, 1959; Gwinn H. Heap, *Central Route to the Pacific,* Philadelphia, 1854, reprint with added documents, Glendale, Calif., 1957; Louis O. Honig, *James Bridger: Pathfinder of the West,* Kansas City, 1951; Overton Johnson and W. H. Winter, *Route across the Rocky Mountains,* Lafayette, Ind., 1846, and Princeton, 1932; Charles Lindsay, *The Big Horn Basin,* Lincoln, 1932; Moses Schallenberger, *The Opening of the California Trails,* Berkeley, 1953; Maurice S. Sullivan, *Travels of Jedediah Smith,* Santa Ana, Calif., 1934, and *Jedediah Smith, Trader and Trail Breaker,* New York, 1936; George R. Stewart, *The Cali-fornia Trail,* New York, 1962.

ern economics, his understanding of social problems and his proficiency as a public office-holder were in combination the foundation of his success, and upon which the structure of his distinction was erected.

Motivating these talents and gifts was great physical energy. Cementing them were the inherent ingredients of ambition, resolution and enterprise. Guiding them was a high intelligence. Supporting them was an unqualified personal courage.

The date of Ashley's birth in Virginia has not been unquestionably established, but available evidence points to the year 1778. Similarly, it has not been determined exactly when he reached Missouri, but the year 1802 appears as the most logical choice. This is deduced from the statement, made by himself in 1831, that he had been acquainted with Missouri problems for twenty-nine years, having resided there before the purchase of Louisiana Territory by the United States. Based on the assumption that these dates are correct, he was twenty-four years of age when the French town of St. Genevieve became his home west of the Mississippi River.

Land and lead mining were the fields which appeared to offer the best prospects, and he entered both. His income was frequently augmented, however, by surveying, a science in which he had received basic training as a youth. Just how he became engaged in mining, whether as a miner or operator, or as both, is not known, but the circumstances of his entrance into the real estate business are not as vague. He married Mary Able, and with his bride came title to considerable land, a present from her father, holder of a Spanish grant. During the next few years he disposed of parts of his land, and bought and sold property in other areas, including St. Louis.

Always looking for additional opportunities to make money, he engaged in several other pursuits, among them a trading trip to the Red River country. The success of this venture prompted him to go east with the intention of expanding his activities as a merchant trader. He bought goods in New York, set sail for New Orleans, and lost them all in a Gulf of Mexico shipwreck. A second project involving an attempt to sell cotton and lead in the East also ended in failure because of depressed prices. In Washington County he engaged in the manufacture of gunpowder, and it was there that some of the first steps which were to lead him to political prominence were taken.

During his activity in mining an event of significance took place. He became a close friend of Andrew Henry, then already celebrated as a fur trader and adventurer.[2] Henry had returned from the mountains in the fall of 1811, and had again taken up lead mining, which he had left to undertake his unsuccessful venture in the far West.

Ashley could not, at the time, have lived in St. Louis, or anywhere else in Missouri, without being fully apprised of events taking place in the fur trade. Yet, there seems little doubt that his serious consideration of it as a field of enterprise for himself developed after he had become a close friend of Henry. The trade was largely dormant during the War of 1812, but with peace came unprecedented activity. Big companies were formed, big expeditions were pushing up the Missouri, big profits were

---

[2] See Part I herein.

being made. These conditions would have excited Ashley, and he would have sought the views and the advice of the experienced Henry, in whom he held implicit faith.

Ashley had been a captain of the state militia as early as 1807, and had resigned. He resumed his military career after the outbreak of the war with Great Britain, again holding a captaincy, and he saw frontier duty for a time in 1813. The next year he became a lieutenant-colonel commanding a new regiment in which Andrew Henry was first major. After the peace he continued to serve and was made a brigadier-general in 1821.

Meanwhile, having established his permanent residence in St. Louis, Ashley continued to devote himself to land speculations and to fulfilling his political ambitions. In 1820 he ran for lieutenant-governor and won election by a few hundred votes. Yet, neither business nor politics were dominating his thoughts at the time. The thoughts were for the most part held in the vise of a daring and unique idea.

For nearly two centuries the fur trade of North America followed the same system of operation. It had been inaugurated by the first French traders to ascend the St. Lawrence, and deviations after that, with two notable exceptions, were inconsequential, of no economic significance.

Brigades pushed up the Ottawa, down the French to Lake Huron, through the Sault Saint Marie, across Lake Superior. Others, using the same route out from Montreal, passed through the Straits of Michillimackinac and into Lake Michigan, to Green Bay and the Fox. Still others opened passages to Lake Ontario and Lake Erie, and found trails southward to the country of the Ohio, southwestward to the Kankakee and the Illinois. The Mississippi was crossed, and the Missouri was found, and the traders pushed up it. Farther north, they were moving through the limitless Canadian forests and onto the western plains. They saw in time the great mountains, and some of them broke through to the Pacific.

Yet, during all this era of discovery and exploration, there were virtually no changes wrought in the trading system under which they opened not only a continent but the richest fur regions in the world. The *voyageurs* and traders established posts and sought to induce the Indians to bring furs to them. Contingents were sent into the wilderness, not to trap but to trade goods for furs. The furs obtained in these ways were held at the permanent posts. Once a year the posts received supplies, transported to them by brigades which left such places as Montreal, Albany, Pittsburgh, New Orleans, St. Louis. The brigades returned in the late summer to their headquarters with the furs taken during the preceding fall and spring.

From Hudson's Bay to Santa Fe, from the Alleghenies to the Columbia, the trade was conducted along these set lines. Yet, its drawbacks were numerous and well understood. Permanent posts were not only expensive to maintain, but they had to be defended. Indians were generally unreliable as trappers, and they were nomadic and unstable in their customs and habits. Tribal wars, weather and competition affected trade, but the posts could not be moved to offset these contingencies. Frequently temporary posts had to be built and men sent to maintain them to prevent loss of a year's business.

Historians are prone to credit Ashley with originating the rendezvous system. He did not. What he did do was to recognize its potentialities, realize its advantages over old orthodox methods, and adapt it successfully to his own needs.

However, it would be unreasonable to assume that Henry, as well, did not hold similar views, that he did not advocate its adoption. Henry was as fully conversant with the history of the trade as his partner, and as cognizant of current conditions. Certainly there can be no doubt as to the great value of his efforts to bring success to the plan of operations upon which they had agreed.

That plan was clearly the result of a meeting of their minds, of a merger of two honest and acute intellects. They were fortunate men, for neither could have obtained more valuable counsel than each was capable of supplying the other – on the one hand, knowledge and understanding born of hardship and disaster and death in the wilderness, and on the other hand, the same valuable assets derived from practical training and experience in commerce, industry and finance. Such a combination, its components supporting and counter-balancing each other to form an effective harmonious whole, could hardly have produced anything less than a revolutionary transition in the fur trade of the American West.

The inventor of the rendezvous system was Donald McKenzie, the traitorous Astorian.

Fat, greasy, rough, uncouth and unscrupulous, McKenzie was also a man of great energy and enterprise. He was a veteran of the wilderness trade when, in 1804, he was temporarily ousted from the North West Company, apparently because he was careless about expenditures and tended toward prodigality in the distribution of goods. Astor selected him as a partner in the Pacific Fur Company because of his trading experience and his outstanding knowledge of Indians. If Astor knew that McKenzie was a man of many moods, that these moods influenced both his personal loyalties and his enmities, or if he was aware that in McKenzie hatred and vengeance were as quick to rise as admiration and kindness, he chose to ignore these facts.

For several years after the perfidious capitulation at Astoria, the North West Company found the fur trade in the Columbia Basin far below expectations. The causes were easier to ascertain than to correct. Men sent into the interior to trade with Indians chose to sit around the posts and wait for them to bring in their furs, instead of seeking to bolster business by trips into the wild. The Indians were just as lazy.

North West Company directors obviously acquired new faith in McKenzie. He had been stationed at Fort George, the former Astoria, but in 1816 he was assigned to the interior with orders to rectify the adverse conditions existing there. Above all, McKenzie was to organize brigades to follow the Indians, obtain their furs, and make explorations to find new sources of supply.

McKenzie appointed men of his own choosing to command the established posts, such as Okanagan, Salish House and Spokane House, and then turned his attention to reviving the trade in the Snake River country. No effort to enter this immense area had been made for more than two years, and he set off for it with what the trader, Alexander Ross, described as the most "motley crew" that ever ascended the Columbia. He was gone for more than eighteen months, through the winters of 1816 and 1817 – an expensive expedition, and typical of McKenzie's former methods which had brought him into disfavor with his employers – but eactly where he went or how many furs he obtained has never been disclosed, if, indeed, such records ever existed. However, a good guess might be that he penetrated beyond the Snake watershed to Bear River, the Uintas, and the upper tributaries of the Green.

Costly and long as his explorations were, they provided the information he sought. He had passed through areas immensely rich in furs, not only beaver but deer, otters, foxes, martens, mountain sheep, and even wild horses. He began to formulate a unique plan.

Spokane House had been the designated headquarters for the Snake River trade. McKenzie found it unsuitable for his purposes. He wanted a base in a more strategic location, closer to the sphere of the operations he intended to undertake. His choice of a site was the junction of the Columbia and Walla Walla rivers. There he built Fort Nez Perces, sent a hundred men to occupy it, and placed Alexander Ross in command.

The year 1818 saw the actual beginning of the rendezvous system. McKenzie led a big column into the Snake Country. The men did not go only as traders who would be assigned stations. They went as trappers, although there was nothing to preclude them from trading with Indians if opportunities arose. There was one other great difference between McKenzie's expedition and those of the past: the trapper-traders would be supplied in large part by what in the military would have been called quartermasters, and the contingents which periodically brought out foodstuffs, equipment and trade goods would take back with them the furs collected. The trapper-traders would remain in the wilderness for indefinite terms. Each brigade would be large enough to defend itself against attack by Indians. There would be no permanent posts – except the headquarters on the Columbia. The entire operation would be mobile. Any brigade could be shifted with little effort or expense to meet exigencies or trade opportunities that might arise.

For the next three years, 1819-1821, McKenzie maneuvered large companies through a vast territory, up the Snake, up its countless tributaries in country never before visited by white men, over great mountains to the basin of the Green, and southward at least as far as Bear Lake in the present state of Utah. He negotiated agreements with various tribes, guaranteeing peaceful relations with them. The Indians responded by bringing in their furs while the white men trapped. Profits were immense. A small British tool, such as an awl, might be exchanged for five prime beaver skins probably worth $30 in London. The untouched streams and the countries bordering them yielded astonishing quantities of furs.

It was altogether, however, an extremely expensive operation, for logistics and inefficient organization cut heavily into net returns. Merchandise, equipment and supplies came from England. They reached their destination by two routes. The most feasible, although by far the longest, was by a voyage of six months or more around the Horn, up the Pacific (perhaps with a stop at the Sandwich Islands) to the Columbia, and up that river to the interior, thence by pack animal to the various rendezvous in the wilderness. The other route came by water

and land from Montreal across Canada to the Columbia.
It could be used only a small part of the year. Neverthe-
less, in spite of the hazards and the expenses, McKenzie's
brigades brought in each year more furs than all the rest
of the gigantic Columbia Department of the North West
Company. He departed for Montreal in 1821, the year
that dynamic organization merged with its great antagonist, the Hudson's Bay Company. The new proprietors
didn't consider the system he had invented suitable for
all of the great empire, stretching from the Atlantic to
the Pacific, over which they ruled, but they permitted
it to continue for a few years in the Columbia Department. When the British were forced to give up organized
trade in American territory west of the mountains, as
they had been on the eastern side, McKenzie's innovation
was completely abandoned by them.

Ashley and Henry, poring over their plans, dreaming
their dreams, in St. Louis understandably could harbor
visions that made the blood race, but they were not carried away by them. The course they charted was based
on the best intelligence, the most reliable reports, obtainable. If they were stirred by their ideas, they were influenced and guided most in their decisions by cold
practicality.

How much they knew of the operations of McKenzie
is not a matter of record. However, it would be difficult
to believe they knew nothing at all of the good fortunes
of the North West Company beyond the mountains.
McKenzie had pursued his rendezvous project several
years by the time they had settled on a plan that emulated
it. Such news traveled fast in the fur trade, carried not

only by that mysterious system of communications, the wilderness telegraph, but by official couriers. Messengers and groups of traders were passing back and forth over the Canadian routes during those years. Mails were being carried regularly between Montreal and New York and St. Louis. McKenzie himself reached Montreal in 1821. Whatever the truth, the fact remains that their original operating strategy was strikingly similar to that which McKenzie had conceived and had carried out. It involved sending two keelboats and a large overland company up the Missouri. They would establish a base post, and they had agreed upon the confluence of the Yellowstone and Missouri rivers at the site. The location undoubtedly had been proposed by Henry. He had been there, understood its advantages, and knew its relationships to important trapping areas. The Yellowstone and the Big Horn were main access routes to the mountains, and trails went on t othe Three Forks and over the Continental Divide to the Snake country and the waters of the Columbia. Other trails led southward to the Wind and the Green. They did not forget the Blackfeet, but retained the hope that they would be able to overcome the hatred held by those savage tribesmen for white men and establish profitable trade relations with them. It must have been a distinctly faint hope in Henry, in view of his own terrible experiences at the Three Forks, but even Ashley, who had never been there, must have known strong misgivings when he considered the matter. However, if by some remote means peace was effected, they would be in a good position to take quick advantage of it. The Missouri was the main highway to the heart of the Blackfoot country, and the first company to

build a fort at the Great Falls might well control the
trade.

The Ashley-Henry plan as originally conceived, therefore, called for the establishment of a base post which
would be supplied by cargo boats traveling up the Missouri River from St. Louis. From the post supplies and
merchandise would be transported by horses to the trapping brigades in the mountains at specified places of
rendezvous. The pack train would bring the furs which
the trappers had collected back to the post, from which
they would be sent down the river.

Things didn't work out as planned, and drastic revisions soon had to be made. It was with these revisions,
however, that Ashley brought the rendezvous system to
its highest degree of effectiveness, and made both it and
himself famous.

The advertisement appeared – it would be followed by
others during the year – and their licenses were granted
by Secretary of War John C. Calhoun, and the equipment and trade merchandise and guns and lead and foodstuffs mounted in their headquarters. The daring men
who would go on the first expedition waited impatiently
for the signal that would send the big keelboat into the
current, snubby prow pointed toward the Missouri's
yellow torrent, and start the pack train on the trail
westward.

The excitement generated by the preparations for the
departure would be long remembered, and there would
be different opinions expressed of both Ashley's plans
and the characters and capabilities of the men he had
engaged.

Years later, after Ashley had died, a writer in the *Missouri Saturday News* would recall that

> These men were well selected from among the numerous applicants for employment; and his [Ashley's] thorough knowledge of character enabled him to embody much efficiency in his first outfit, and in the subsequent additions which he made to his company. . . Armed and equipped fitly for desperate encounters with the red man, or his genial spirit the grizzly bear, these men paraded the streets while putting the last finish to desperate preparations. Like the reckless crew of a man-of-war about to cruise against the enemy's squadron, they indulged deeply in the luxuries they might never again realize. The generous impulses which mark the character of such brave men, were extensively developed before their departure   .   .   .

It was a polite way of saying that they got drunk, cavorted with sluts, and yowled their way from saloon to saloon, but the writer might well have mentioned that some of them took time out from their labors and their carousing to kneel in candlelight before the altar of the little church Bishop Duborg had erected on Rue de la Tour, only a few staggers from the bistros of Rue Royale and the riverfront.

Thomas Hempstead, a partner of the Missouri Fur Company, didn't think too well of either Ashley's plan or his men. He wrote Joshua Pilcher, his colleague who was on the upper river, that

> the men are all generally speaking untried and of every description and nation. . . the Company will be conducted by honourable men, I think, but I expect they will wish nothing more of us than to unite in case of difficulty.   my opinion as regards the manner that those men are employed

might differ with yours, but I think it will not. they are engaged in three different ways I am told the hunters and trapers are to have one half of the furs &c they make the company furnish them with Gun Powder Lead &c &c, they only are to help to build the fort & defend it in case of necessity. the boat hands are engaged as we engage ours. the Clerks are also the same but of those are the fewest number. I do think when men are engaged upon the principals of the above, that regularity, subordination, system which is highly necessary to have on that river should be the first object of any company to establish, but pray let me ask you in what way it can be done under those circumstances. Should the hunters wish after they get above to leave them in a mass in what way will they prevent them, this kind of business of making hunters will take time and much trouble.

The first boat and overland party, commanded by Major Henry, got away from St. Louis early in April, 1822, and the *St. Louis Enquirer,* hailing the event with a sincere *bon voyage,* reported: "The object of this company is to trap and hunt – they are completely equipped, and number about 180 persons. They will direct their course to the three forks of the Missouri, a region, it is said, which contains a wealth in Furs, not surpassed by the mines of Peru. The party is composed entirely of young men, many of whom have relinquished the most respectable employments and circles of society, for this arduous but truly meritorious undertaking." A few days later the *Missouri Intelligencer* added its wishes of good fortune to the announcement that "the party arrived at Franklin on Thursday last, and have proceeded to their destination. We wish every success to so arduous an undertaking, & sincerely hope it may be productive of individual gain as well as of public advantage."

Ashley got his second boat, with Daniel S. D. Moore in charge, away on May 8, 1822, approximately a month after the first had departed. The delay had been caused by the unavailability of certain articles of equipment, notably some guns which were being brought out to him from Pennsylvania.

Two of the trappers engaged for the first Ashley-Henry expedition properly deserve special notice at this time, for they would soon acquire unsurpassed fame as explorers and traders – as Mountain Men.

One was a strapping youngster of eighteen. He had been born in Richmond, Virginia, in 1804, the son of a tavern keeper. When he was eight years old his family had moved to Missouri and had settled on a farm in Six Mile Prairie. At thirteen he had been apprenticed to a St. Louis blacksmith. He had continued in this work, also doing odd jobs on the waterfront, for the next five years. Then had come the fateful day when he heard of the advertisement – he couldn't read – and was accepted as an "Ashley man." His name was James Bridger.

The other young man was twenty-three years of age, a native of Chenango County, New York. As a youth he had been taught to read and write by a physician who recognized his keen intellect and studious turn of mind. His family migrated from the Mohawk Valley in several moves, over a period of years. He was eighteen when they settled in St. Louis. A desire to explore the western wilderness, which began only a few miles away, quickly developed. His opportunity came in the winter of 1822. He not only could read the Ashley advertisement, but he could write about answering it. His name was Jedediah Strong Smith.

Smith left for posterity a journal of inestimable value. Without it many of the most dramatic events in western history would have had no chronicler. These words, which he wrote in the spring of 1822, are a case in point:

> Leaving St. Louis our boat proceded on without any material occurrence for the first three hundred miles. The strong current of the Missouri made the voyage slow Laborious and dangerous. Arrived at a place within the state of Missouri and near the mouth of the Sni Eber [Sniabar] Creek on a windy day and turning a point full of sawyers the boat by an unexpected turn brought the top of her mast against a tree that hung over the water and wheeling with the side to the powerful current was swept under in a moment.

The big keelboat, weighing perhaps twelve tons, and its heavy cargo, valued at $10,000 in St. Louis and many times that amount on the upper Missouri, were devoured so swiftly by the mighty river that many of the men on board narrowly escaped. The post-mortem was quickly concluded. After establishing a camp, Moore, presumably with two or three boatmen, set out for St. Louis in a canoe.

The scene of the disaster was near the present city of Lexington, Missouri, approximately 340 miles from St. Louis by river. It had taken the keelboat three weeks to reach it. Moore and his paddlers made the return trip in less than six days.

Jedediah Smith wrote that Ashley was "not discouraged" by the bad news. That hardly seem plausible. Ashley was not in a position to take lightly the loss of an investment of such proportions. In Missouri in the year 1822, few men were in that position. Ashley's reaction, however, could have given such an impression. He did not lose his courage, but that is quite different from saying that he was not profoundly discouraged.

Moore had no sooner made his sad report than Ashley was at work organizing a third boat. It was an illustration of the man's measure. Credit for merchandise and equipment was not a problem, an indisputable indication of his reputation as a businessman and the confidence merchants had in him.

In the remarkably short time of eighteen days he recruited a new company of men, bought another keelboat, loaded it with cargo, and, taking command himself, started up the river.

Had he been able to look at all into the future, he might well have been dismayed to the extent that he would have abandoned the entire enterprise.

The story of Ashley and Henry in the next two years is one of extreme hardships, bitter disappointments and stark tragedies. They seemed to have been cursed by an evil omen. Misfortunes dogged them. Men of lesser stature, of less determination, of less faith than they had in themselves, of less fortitude, would surely have surrendered to the diabolical forces pursuing them.

Andrew Henry's boat, Number One, and the accompanying land train were above the Mandan Villages in August 1822. They had met with no serious mishap in their journey of more than sixteen hundred miles up the river. Then they were struck a severe blow. A large band of Assiniboines, making signs of friendship, approached the shore party. Through clever maneuvering they were able to make off with fifty horses.

Badly crippled and its plans for a fall hunt disrupted by the loss, the company pressed on with increased speed to the mouth of the Yellowstone. The site chosen for a post was on a tongue of land on the right bank of the Missouri, about a quarter of a mile above the confluence. As soon as the building was erected, Henry dispatched several parties with two missions each – to obtain furs and secure more horses. Both were performed with moderate success among the Crows.

Meanwhile, Boat Number Three, having picked up the company from the wrecked Boat Number Two, had pushed steadily up the river. Jedediah Smith recorded that it reached the Arikara Villages on September 8th, and that Ashley "determined as the season was much advanced to purchase horses and proceed directly by land to the Mouth of the Yellow stone whilst the boat which would proceed more slowly would continue on to the same place."

Smith was assigned to the land party, which Ashley led. The course followed took them north-northwest across the great rolling plains from the Grand River to the Mandan Villages. Thence they traveled generally northwest, not far from the Missouri, crossing the Heart, the Knife and the Little Missouri, which Smith described as "remarkable even in comparison with the Large river for its muddy turbid waters." Henry's post at the mouth of the Yellowstone was reached on October first.

The air was sharp with the feel of fall, and the northern river might soon be closed to travel by winter. Ashley spent only a few days at the post. It was agreed that Henry would remain in command while Ashley returned to St. Louis and made arrangements to bring out in the spring two more boats, enough supplies to last a year, and another hundred men. Meanwhile, trapping and trading parties would be sent out, and all furs obtained would be brought into the post where they could be picked up by the 1823 boats.

Ashley departed on his homeward journey in a large perogue. He was accompanied by several experienced rivermen, and he took with him the furs which had been collected since Henry's company had reached the Yellowstone. Ice was floating in the Missouri before he had passed the Council Bluffs.

The trapping parties went out from Fort Henry as planned, and Henry himself led a small company up the Missouri into the heart of the Blackfoot country. This was a venture which Henry, if he thought at all about his own disastrous experiences at the hands of these Indians, might not have been expected to undertake. It seems apparent that nothing could prevent him from attempting to invade the fabulously rich region. Certainly no fear he held, if he held any at all, could overcome his determination to make money.

Henry was soon followed by another group of which Jedediah Smith was a member. According to Smith they "ascended the Missouri traveling immediately along the bank of the river. . . On our way up we met Maj Henry on his return."

Henry went back to the post at the Yellowstone, and Smith and his men continued up the Missouri, and "About the first of November we arrived at the mouth of the Muscle Shell River which was the place of our destination."

Eight of them decided they did not like the prospect

of spending the long winter virtually trapped among the Blackfeet, and they turned back. The other five built cabins, laid in a supply of meat, and made themselves as comfortable otherwise as possible. Smith felt that in their little encampment "shut out from those enjoyments most valued by the world we were as happy as we could be made by leisure and opportunity for unlimited indulgence in the pleasure of the Buffalo hunt and the several kinds of sport which the severity of the winter could not debar us from."

The ice in the river broke early in April, and the men set out in canoes to trap. On April 11th, one of them, Daniel Potts, was shot through both legs when a rifle was accidentally discharged. He was taken in a canoe, probably by Smith, down to Fort Henry.

At about the same time, Henry set out from the post with seven reinforcements for the trappers on the Musselshell. After the meeting, the party of eleven men began trapping operations a short distance above Smith River. The Blackfeet struck. Four trappers were slain, and the others, abandoning their equipment, which included more than two hundred traps, fled the country. Henry, at last, was convinced of the futility of attempting to establish trade relations with the Blackfeet.

Important events were taking place in St. Louis that spring of 1823. Astor was making his power felt. Big outfits were preparing to go up the rivers, and one of the biggest was that of Ashley and Henry.[3] Another adver-

---

[3]They are generally credited with operating under the name of "Rocky Mountain Fur Company," but they did not. That name properly belongs to a company organized by some of Ashley's successors. Ashley and Henry used only their own names.

tisement had brought more celebrated names to Ashley's payroll – William L. Sublette, Thomas Fitzpatrick, David E. Jackson, to name three of the most outstanding.[4] With a company of a hundred men and two large keelboats, the *Rocky Mountains* and the *Yellow Stone Packet,* Ashley left St. Louis on Monday, March 10, 1823.

The expedition was ill-fated from the moment it started.

"We understand," reported the *Missouri Republican,* "a man fell overboard from one of the boats, on Monday morning, and was drowned."

In a dispatch from St. Charles, headed AFFLICTING OCCURRENCE, the *St. Louis Enquirer* informed its readers:

> On Thursday morning last, three men belonging to general Ashley's expedition to the Yellow Stone, were conveying a quantity of powder in a cart to the boats at St. Charles, and had proceeded scarcely a half mile from this place, when fire was communicated to the powder by means of a pipe. [Presumably a pipe being smoked by one of the men.] The explosion was tremendous and produced a concussion similar to that of a slight earthquake. The men were blown into the air to the height of several hundred feet, the cart shivered to pieces, and the horses much injured. One of the men survived a few minutes after his descent to the ground; the others were entirely lifeless and burnt in the most shocking manner. The quantity of the powder in the cart before the explosion took place exceeded three hundred pounds.

James Clyman, who would win a certain distinction beyond the frontier, held a low opinion of Ashley's re-

---

[4] Ashley advertised for men in three newspapers: *Missouri Gazette and Public Advertiser,* Feb. 13 to Mar. 6; *Missouri Republican,* Mar. 20 and 27; and *St. Louis Enquirer,* Feb. 26 to Mar. 22, 1822.

cruits, and told his diary: "A description of our crew
I cannt give but Fallstafs Battallion was genteel in com-
parison. . . Two Keel Boats with crews of French some
St. Louis gumboes as they ware called."

A few days later, when still among the farms and
settlements of the lower river, the boats were held up
by high winds. Wrote Clyman: "The men went out
gunning and that night came in with plenty of game
Eggs Fowls Turkeys and what not. Haveing a fire on
shore they dressed cooked and eat untill midnight being
care full to burn all the fragments. . . in the morning
several Neighbours came in hunting for poultry. Liberty
was given to search the boats but they found nothing
and left." A short time later, after the boats had gone
some distance, sails were raised "when out droped pigs
and poultry in abundance."

Clyman wrote that eight or ten men elected to leave
the expedition at Fort Atkinson and enlist in the army,
and that two or three soldiers whose enlistments had ex-
pired entered the service of Ashley. As the boats passed
through the Sioux country distressing reports were received. Arikara raiders had attacked trading posts of
the Missouri Fur Company and had stolen a considerable
amount of merchandise, furs and horses. Two warriors
had been killed and a number wounded.

Forewarned in this way, Ashley advanced with guns
ready. As he neared the Arikara Villages, at the mouth
of Grand River, an intrepid Jed Smith arrived with a
message from Henry recounting the difficulties encountered in the Blackfoot country and telling of the urgent
need for more horses at Fort Henry. Ashley at once
planned to obtain the animals from the Arikaras and

dispatch them with reinforcements to the post on the Yellowstone. The month of May was ending when the expedition came in sight of the first Arikara village.

During the next week Ashley would pen several letters and reports as he waited to be rescued from the perilous position into which he had been driven. He had lost more than half the strength of his company of ninety men – at least a dozen dead, six dangerously wounded and more than thirty by desertion. He had retreated down the river some twenty-five or thirty miles and established a camp in a thick wood, which would provide added protection in the event of another attack. One of his boats, carrying forty-three wounded and deserters, had been sent down the river to Fort Atkinson, near the Council Bluffs. Ashley also had sent an urgent express to the commandment, Colonel Henry Leavenworth, requesting troops to support him. He had called for volunteers to carry a letter to Henry on the Yellowstone, and the indefatigable Jed Smith had responded. The letter ordered Henry to descend the river with all possible reinforcements.

A few excerpts from Ashley's writing not only provide a graphic picture of the fight but make more understandable events which followed. The disaster, more than anything else occurring in the wilderness at the time, brought about abrupt changes in his operations, changes that were greatly influential on the course of the fur trade in the days immediately ahead.

To the *Missouri Republican* Ashley wrote:

> On the morning of the 2nd inst. (June) I was attacked by the Ricaree Indians, which terminated seriously on my

part. . . Not one of the Ricaree Indians did I see until I
arrived at their towns, on the 30th of May; my boats were
anchored about the middle of the river, and I went on shore
with two men where I met with some of the principal chiefs
who pretended to be very friendly disposed toward us, and
expressed a wish that I should trade with them.

Wishing to send a party through by land from that point
to the Yellow Stone river, for which purpose forty or fifty
horses were necessary and having just received an express
from Major Henry, sent for the purpose of desiring me to
purchase all the horses I could on my way, I consented to
send some goods on shore to exchange for horses, but proposed that the chiefs of the two towns would meet me on
the sand beach, where a perfect understanding should take
place before the barter commenced. After a long consul-
tation among them, they appeared at the place to hold the
talk. I made them a small present, which appeared to please
them very much. . .

By the end of the day, June 1, Ashley had obtained
the horses he wanted, and planned to leave with them
for the Yellowstone the next morning. Several of his men,
perhaps seeking female companionship, apparently had
remained in the village without Ashley's permission.
Shortly before dawn he was awakened and informed that
one man had been killed and that an attack on the boats
was imminent.

.   .   .   my party consisted of ninety men, forty of whom
were selected to accompany me to the Yellow Stone river
by land, and were encamped on the sand beach in charge
of the horses.

About sun rise the Indians commenced a heavy and well
directed fire from a line extending along the picketing of one
their towns and some broken ground adjoining, a distance
of about six hundred yards. Seeing that some of the horses

were killed and others wounded, as well as two or three
men, I attempted to have the horses crossed to a sand bar
about the middle of the river, over which the water was
about three feet deep, but before any thing to effect that
object could be done, the fire became very destructive, aimed
principally at the men on shore. I ordered the anchor weighed
and the boats put to shore but the boatmen, with but very
few exceptions were so panic struck that they could not be
got to execute the order. Two skiffs which would carry thirty
men, were taken a shore for the embarcation of the men
but (I suppose) from a predetermination of the men on the
beach not to give way to the Indians as long as there appeared the least possibility of keeping their ground, not more
than five of them made use of the large skiff two of whom
were wounded, the other skiff was taken to the other side of
the river by two men, one of them mortally wounded.

   . . . by this time the most of the horses were killed
or wounded and about half of the men, I continued to make
every effort to get the boats to shore but all in vain, although
anchored not more than ninety feet out in the stream the
most of the men swan to the boats, some of them when
shot immediately sprang into the river and sunk. It was
about fifteen minutes from the time the firing commenced
until the surviving part of the men had embarked. The
anchor of one of the boats was weighed the cable of the
other cut, and the boats dropped down the stream.

The following day Ashley proposed that another attempt to pass the villages in boats be made, but "to my
great surprise and mortification, when my intentions were
made known to the men I was informed that (with but
few exceptions,) they would desert me, if I attempted
it, and that however well the boats might be fortified
they would not make a second attempt to pass without
a large reinforcement."

In his appeal for troops, Ashley informed Indian Agent

Benjamin O'Fallon and Colonel Leavenworth at the
Council Bluffs that the Arikara warriors numbered about
six hundred and "I suppose that three fourths of them
armed with London Fuzils."

In a letter to a friend, Ashley said: "To describe my
feelings at seeing these men destroyed, is out of my
power. . . How many of the enemy were killed I cannot
tell, but suppose not more than six or eight. Four or
five were seen to fall on the beach."

Four days after he received Ashley's call for help,
Colonel Leavenworth was ascending the Missouri River
at the head of more than two hundred infantrymen. They
had with them two six-pounders and several small swivel
guns. This force was augmented by a heavily armed
contingent from the posts of the Missouri Fur Company
led by its president, Joshua Pilcher, and by more than
three hundred Indian recruits, most of them Sioux eager
to participate in any campaign against the hated Arikaras.
Henry and his trappers from the Yellowstone were waiting with Ashley when, after a trip of forty-eight days,
Leavenworth's column arrived. On August 9th, the attack on the villages, led by the Sioux, was begun.

Details of the Leavenworth engagement with the Arikaras have no bearing on the subject being treated in
this book. The result of it do.

As far as having any lasting effect, the campaign was
a failure. Leavenworth showed himself to be inept. His
unwillingness to make decisions so disgusted the Sioux
that, after stealing the Arikara's corn, they departed.
Following a parley with some Arikara leaders, in which
he received their promise to behave, Leavenworth asked
Pilcher to draw up a treaty. Furious at the turn of

affairs, Pilcher refused. It was his contention that only by severely chastising the Arikaras could peace between traders and the upper river tribes be assured. Leavenworth next requested Henry to write the treaty. He, too, refused. At last, Leavenworth prepared it himself, and the peace pipe was smoked.

The Mountain Men understood that in the Indian way of thinking peace without victory was not peace at all. The white men – and the United States army – had conducted a comic opera campaign. They had been humbled. They had actually begged for peace. The warriors were laughing at them. More blood would have to run before the issue was resolved.

A provision of Leavenworth's treaty required the Arikaras to restore all property taken from Ashley – horses, guns, merchandise and equipment. They restored one horse, three rifles and sixteen buffalo robes, then, during the night, vanished. Leavenworth sent messengers to find them and ask them to return to their villages, but they had disappeared into the great plains.

Leavenworth then decided the Arikaras had been sufficiently frightened and would not commit further depredations against the traders. He turned back downstream with his force. Almost before he had got out of sight the villages were fired by Missouri Fur Company men.

There would be no peace on the Missouri with the Arikaras. A prophecy made by Pilcher would prove to be accurate. "It is my sincere and candid opinion," he wrote Indian Agent O'Fallon only a few days after the troops had departed, "that the expedition against the Aricaras from which so much services might have been rendered to this dwindling and bleeding commerce, will

rather tend to increase, than diminish, the evil; that the
situation of affairs in this country is worsted materially;
that instead of raising the American character in the
estimation of its inhabitants and impressing them with
the power and spirit of our government, the contrary effect has been produced; and that the outrages of the
Indians will increase in consequence." O'Fallon expressed similar views in a letter to the War Department.

His own outburst and O'Fallon's support, however,
did not satisfy Pilcher. He sent an abusive letter to
Leavenworth in which he stated: "You came (to use
your own language) to 'open and make this great road';
instead of which you have, by the imbecility of your conduct and operations, created and left impossible barriers."

The failure of Leavenworth to open the upper Missouri for safe travel by trading parties brought not only
severe disruption of the river commerce, but a corollary
result upon which historical accounts generally have
failed to turn the bright light it deserves. The military
debacle made unmistakably apparent the remarkable
elasticity of the plan—the system, if you please—which
Ashley had set in motion.

Within a few days after the soldiers had disappeared
down the river, he had formulated drastic revisions in
the program he had intended to carry out. If he could
not send his company up the river, he was not to be
precluded from continuing his enterprise by other means
and in other ways. Had he been dependent upon permanent posts on the Missouri, he would, in all probability,
have suffered the loss of a year's trade.

Ashley and his men dropped down the river to Fort
Kiowa, above the mouth of the White River. There he

equipped Henry and thirty men and sent them overland to the post on the Yellowstone. Next he organized a company, to be led by Jedediah Smith, which was to travel directly west to the Crow Country. There it would be joined by a party which Henry would send up the Big Horn. Trapping would be carried on during the fall, winter and spring, and goods would be sent out to them, by the Missouri or overland, whichever route was deemed the most advantageous at the time.

This was the actual beginning of the rendezvous system as it was practiced by Ashley. He had made an attempt to establish it by working out of the advance post on the Yellowstone. It was clear to him now that this plan was infeasible and presented excessive dangers. He abandoned it, and began to think in terms of supplying his men directly in the wilderness, although as yet he had not settled on a specific place for the first rendezvous. That would be done as soon as possible.

Ashley's wisdom and foresight were amply illustrated by the experiences of Henry's company of some thirty men which set out from Fort Kiowa in September 1823. A few days after starting they were set upon by Indians, believed to be Grosventres. The raiders killed two trappers, wounded two, and made off with two horses. Upon reaching Fort Henry, they found that more than a score of the horses left there had been stolen by Blackfeet. Seven more animals were spirited away by raiders a few days later.

Henry had reached the conclusion that the site was untenable, and loading furs and goods into a keelboat, he started up the Yellowstone. Near the mouth of the Powder he fortunately met Crows from whom he obtained

forty-seven horses. This enabled him to start two parties
for the mountains. One continued on up the Yellowstone,
taking pelts in various tributaries. The other went up
the Big Horn and reached Wind River. Henry continued
on to the confluence of the Big Horn and Yellowstone,
where he erected another post.

With Jedediah Smith when he left the Missouri, following the Arikara fight, were seventeen men. It was
during the winter and the following spring that this band,
and other groups from the post at the mouth of the Big
Horn, wrote a great saga of exploration. South Pass was
discovered. The mountains were crossed, and both the
Salt Lake Basin and the Snake country were penetrated.

During the winter a camp had been established in a
grove at the lower end of Sweetwater Canyon. They remained there for several weeks, subsisting mainly on
mountain sheep. When they again started out in several
small parties to trap, they left a cache of powder, lead
and other articles. It was agreed that they would assemble at the cache early in June.

This was the first prearranged American rendezvous
in the mountains. From it the furs were taken to the Big
Horn, loaded on boats, and Henry set off with them for
St. Louis.

On August 30th, 1824, the *St. Louis Enquirer* reported that Henry had arrived "with a considerable quantity of valuable furs, &c." The actual value of the cargo
was known only to its proprietors, but it could not have
been great, for in the fall of 1824, Ashley and Henry were
insolvent and on the verge of bankruptcy.

Henry had had enough of the mountains. Since the

year 1810, when he had led his beaten and hungry band out of the Three Forks and across the Continental Divide to establish the first American post on Pacific waters, he had dreamed of growing rich from beaver skins. Always fortune had eluded him. Instead, he had known only hardship and failure. Now, his dream shattered, his hope gone, he gave up.

Deeply in debt and facing ruin, Ashley characteristically refused to surrender. If his faith in his great scheme was shaken, it was far from destroyed, and now the reputation he had maintained for so many years as a man of high principle and integrity stood him in good stead. However, perhaps this was not the only reason his suppliers agreed to extend him more credit. If he had gone into bankruptcy, he would have pulled them down with him.

Although he had already determined to carry on, receipt of a letter from Thomas Fitzpatrick, who had gone out with Jedediah Smith from Fort Kiowa following the disaster at the Arikara Villages, brought welcome encouragement. The regions which had been explored beyond South Pass, said Fitzpatrick, were rich in beaver.

Ashley's resolution and enthusiasm would not permit him to wait until spring to start westward. Early in October 1824, he was at the head of a pack train – twenty-five men, fifty horses, one wagon and team (it was soon abandoned) – well on the way to Fort Atkinson. On Christmas day the little band was making its way slowly up the South Platt in bitter cold and deep snow.

Ignoring every warning from military men, traders and Indians that to attempt to cross the plains and mountains in winter could bring only disaster and death, Ashley started out. It was more than a bold venture. It was the daring act of a man driven by an uncontrolable determination to succeed, a man who could defy all odds, take all chances, risk his own life and the last outfit he would be able to obtain in his bankrupt condition.

The hazardous expedition, during which he and his men suffered extreme hardships, brought to Ashley glory as one of the greatest of western explorers. He and his men were the first to travel the South Platte route to the mountains in winter. They crossed the Continental Divide by the variation of the South Pass that would bear the name of James Bridger. They penetrated the ranges of the region that would become northern Colorado. They reached the Great Basin. They explored the terrifying canyons of Green River. They were the first to accomplish all of these feats.

Jedediah Strong Smith would go on, on through the unknown deserts to the Pacific coast, the first American to mark out a southern and then a central route across the continent.

Late in April 1825, Ashley and his trappers were encamped on Green River, near the mouth of the Sandy.[5] There an event of great significance in the history of the American fur trade of the Far West occurred. In his narrative of the expedition and in his personal diary, Ashley tells of it in these words:

> . . . arrangements made for starting to make our hunt. . . I will transport the goods and extra baggage down the river [by boat] to some conspicuous point . . . the place of deposit will be made on or near the river. . . The place of deposit as aforesaid, will be *The place of randavose*

---

[5] The western end of Sweetwater County, Wyoming.

for all our parties on or before the 10th of July next &
that the place may be known – Trees will be peeled. . .
should such a point be without timber I will raise a mound
of Earth five feet high or Set up rocks the top of which will
be made red with vermillion thirty feet distant from the
same – and one foot below the surface of the earth a northwest direction will be deposited a letter communicating to
the parties any thing I may deem necessary . . .

. . . all things being ready for our departure, I dispatched six men northwardly to the sources of the river;
seven others set out for a mountain bearing s.s.w. and n.n.e.,
a distance about thirty miles; and six others were sent in a
southern direction. . . they were instructed to endeavor to
fall in with two parties of men that were fitted out by me
in the year previous, and who were then, as I supposed,
beyond the range of mountains appearing westwardly. The
partisans were also informed that I would descend the river
to some eligible point . . . there deposit a part of
my merchandise, and make such marks as would designate
it as a place of *General Rendezvous* for the men in my
service in that country, and where they were all directed
to assemble on or before the 10th of July following.

. . . I embarked with six men . . . on board
my newly made boat and began the descent of the river.

Just south of the boundary of the present states of
Wyoming and Utah, Henry's Fork pours its clear mountain torrent into Green River. It was near this confluence
that Ashley, in the spring of 1825, cached his supplies
and equipment, and made the marks that established it
as his place of *General Rendezvous*.

Out of the wilderness, in the first days of July, came
the trappers. Men were there whose names would be
long remembered, such names as Ephraim Logan,

Thomas Virgin, Etienne Provost, Johnson Gardner, Gabriel Prudhomme, Alexander Carson, James Bridger, Jedediah Smith, James Clyman, William Sublette, Thomas Fitzpatrick, Zachariah Ham, John H. Weber, David E. Jackson, Robert Campbell, James P. Beckwourth—to name but a few. Ashley wrote that one hundred and twenty assembled. They were not all men he had sent out. The total included at least twenty-nine deserters from the Hudson's Bay Company brigades operating in the Snake River basin and elsewhere, and a number of free-trappers, who sold him their furs. The extent of the journeys made by these men may be judged from Ashley's statement that "we had been scattered over the territory west of the mountains in small detachments from the 38th to 44th degree of latitude." It was a slight exaggeration, perhaps a degree of two too far to the south, but if he had said "40th to 44th," it would have been astounding enough—from Utah Lake to Jackson Hole, from the Green to the Snake.

The exact location of the rendezvous has never been determined. Jim Beckwourth stated that the goods were "uncached" at the mouth of Henry's Fork, and then Ashley's men "moved up the river" to a point where the Canadians had agreed to meet them. He did not say which river, the Green or Henry's Fork. Ashley reported that the rendezvous took place "about 20 miles distant" from the cache, but he did not give the direction.

The lack of information is regrettable, for an historical monument certainly should mark the site.

Beckwourth wrote that the rendezvous continued for eight days. Perhaps some of the trappers remained that long. Ashley's narrative records that he was there only two days, which seems quite unlikely. He could hardly have got his accounts in order and have completed innumerable necessary transactions in that time. He wrote that he started home on July 2, but he was often mistaken in his dates.

Accuracy in this instance is of little consequence. What is more important is that when he left the rendezvous he took with him at least one hundred packs of prime Rocky Mountain beaver, the finest in the world.[6]

---

[6] Several histories and early-day accounts state that in the spring of 1825 Ashley came into possession of an immense quantity of furs under peculiar circumstances. Many essential details of the episode are lacking, and the stories about it are conflicting in important respects. But of one vital fact there can be no doubt: some of Ashley's trappers were involved, and the furs in question belonged to a Hudson's Bay Company band commanded by the noted Peter Skene Ogden.

In his *History of the American Fur Trade,* Chittenden has this to say, "At some point north of Great Salt Lake, and possibly in the beautiful mountain park of Cache Valley, an event took place which marked the turning point in Ashley's fortunes. There was in this neighborhood at this time (1825) a party of Hudson Bay trappers under the leadership of the well-known trader, Peter Skeen [sic] Ogden. They were in possession of a large quantity of beaver fur variously estimated at from seventy to two hundred thousand dollars' worth. These furs, through some transaction not now positively known, came into Ashley's possession at an insignificant price — some say by looting a cache in which they were concealed, and some by voluntary sale to Ashley by Ogden to relieve the latter's necessities. Be that as it may, the event was an important one to Ashley."

In a footnote Chittenden adds, "Common tradition among the traders . . . says that Ashley and Provost accidentally came upon a cache of Ogden's fur, and not feeling very well disposed toward the British on general principles, nor believing that they had any business in this quarter [American territory], promptly confiscated the fur. One authority says that Ogden was in great straits for some cause or other, and that he sold out to Ashley for a mere nominal sum in order to relieve his necessities."

Chittenden quotes the trader, Nathaniel Wyeth, as saying that a "Mr. Gardner, one of his [Ashley's] agents, met a Mr. Ogden, clerk of the H.B.Co. in the Snake country at the head of a trapping party. [Johnson] Gardner induced the men of Ogden's party to desert by promises of supplies and good prices for furs. The furs thus obtained amounted to about

It would have been faster and more direct to have traveled from the Green by way of the South Pass and the Platte route to St. Louis, but all available horses were needed by the trappers who would remain in the mountains, and he pointed his packtrain for the mouth of the Big Horn.

"I set out on my way homewards," he said in his

---

130 packs, or 13,000 pounds, worth at that time about $75,000." Chittenden also credits James Beckwourth, an Ashley man, with the statement that the furs cost Ashley "comparatively little." Then Chittenden comments, "That Ogden should voluntarily dispose of his furs at all, and particularly at a nominal price to an American rival, is scarcely creditable to one who knows anything of the business methods of the British companies."

On July 26, 1825, John Work, the Hudson's Bay Company factor at Fort Okanogan, recorded in his journal: "A series of misfortunes have attended the party [Ogden's] from shortly after their departure, and, on the 24th of May they fell in with a party of Americans when twenty-three of the former deserted."

Harrison C. Dale says in his *Ashley-Smith Explorations* that the Hudson's Bay men "not only deserted but took all their furs with them, disposing of them to Ashley's men . . ."

The actual desertion of Ogden's men occurred on the Weber River, a considerable distance south of Cache Valley. At the time, Ashley was returning from his disastrous exploration of the Green River, and he could not have been at the scene. However, he would pass within thirty miles of it late in June, and he would mention in his diary that he was hoping to meet Johnson Gardner, his man who assertedly had induced the Ogden trappers to desert.

Dale L. Morgan in his *West of William Ashley* notes that when Ashley was near the confluence of Chalk Creek and the Weber River: "Less than a month before, on May 23-25, down this very canyon and within thirty miles of where Ashley was now encamped, Johnson Gardner, a leading free trapper, had incited twenty-three of Peter Skene Ogden's men to desert, a stroke which forced Ogden into headlong retreat back to the Snake River. Provost had been on the scene at the time, and must have given Ashley a full account of this dramatic occurrence. Ogden's deserters had taken with them seven hundred beaver, so Ashley understandably would be anxious to fall in with Gardner."

Very true. And Ashley did "fall in" with Gardner. Ashley's accounts show that Gardner delivered a considerable number of beaver pelts to him

narrative, "with 50 men, 25 of whom were to accompany me to a navigable point of the Big Horn River thence to return with the horses employed in the transportation of the furs."

He could not have known that on the Yellowstone he would find a military expedition commanded by General Henry Atkinson and Major Benjamin O'Fallon, which had come up the Missouri during the summer. When he

---

at the rendezvous on Henry's Fork. The Hudson's Bay Company deserters — 29 not 23 — also were at the rendezvous, and it can only be presumed that their furs were duly delivered into Ashley's hands.

More than two years later, on October 17, 1827, the *Missouri Observer* reported that Ashley had received furs from the Rocky Mountains "probably worth $60,000 or $70,000," and went on to remark that "Gen. Ashley in his first expedition in the year 1825, fell in with one of these British parties which had fur in its possession to the value of $200,000."

Ashley obviously felt that the story contained certain implications which might be misunderstood, and he took the trouble to write the editor. His letter, which appeared in the *Observer* on October 31, said: "Permit me to correct an error in your editorial remarks of the 17th instant, noticing the arrival of my mountain expedition at St. Louis. It appears from the statement, that I met a party of British traders west of the Rocky Mountains in the year 1825, who had with them two hundred thousand dollars worth of furs. I saw some of the men who had been of the party alluded to, after they had detached themselves from it, but did not see Mr. Ogden (the partizan), or any of the men who remained with him. I was informed, however, that they had about six thousand pounds of beaver with them at that time, and that in the course of several hunts which they had made upon our Territory west of the Rocky mountains, they had taken about eighty-five thousand beaver, say, 150,000 pounds; worth about *six hundred thousand dollars!*

"Some of the American hunters, who were then, and others who had been, in my employ, went to the British camp, which consisted of about sixty men in the service of the Hudson Bay Company. The circumstances which produced this visit had nearly led to serious consequences. Messrs. Jedediah S. Smith, Wm. L. Sublette and several others of the American party, intelligent young men, of strict veracity, had visited the British camp and reported to their comrades, that the British flag had been repeatedly hoisted during their stay there. The Americans, indignant at such impertinence and understanding, too, that the British camp was within eight miles

reached them they were preparing to return downstream, and they offered to transport his men and his furs.

The wheel of fortune had turned for William H. Ashley. In early October he was in St. Louis.

"It is thus," cried the *Missouri Advocate* with obvious pride, "by the effort of heroic enterprize, Genl. Ashley has indemnified himself for all the losses occasioned by the murderous attack of the Arikaras in the summer of the year 1823."

Not only the losses caused by the Arikaras' attack, but all others as well – the loss of the loaded keelboat, the losses in the Blackfoot country – and all his debts to the trading houses of St. Louis could be repaid. Moreover, even after that had been done, there would be money

---

of them, resolved to proceed to the place and tear down the flag, even at the risk of their lives. Twenty-two of them, with the American flag hoisted, advanced to the spot, but no British flag was to be seen. They made known their business to Mr. Ogden, and protested in threatening language against a recurrence of the same insult offered them; they also required of Mr. Ogden to move his party from that vicinity without delay. Mr. O. first hesitated, calling upon his men for protection, but ultimately finding there would probably be much danger in delay, he lost no time in getting under way, and has kept a respectful distance ever since. At the time of this occurrence I was descending the Rio Colorado of the West, but shortly after, returned and joined the party of American hunters, from whom I received the above account."

Seven hundred beaver which the deserters allegedly delivered to Ashley at rendezvous would weigh at least 1,050 pounds, possibly more, although Rocky Mountain beaver were not as large as those taken on the Missouri and in the Great Lakes region. But using the figure of 1,050 — one and one-half pounds each — the value of the skins in St. Louis would have been $5,250.

Wyeth, it will be recalled, stated that the deserters delivered to Ashley's men 13,000 pounds valued at $75,000.

All that can be said is that there is a lot of beaver between $5,250 and $75,000. Ashley confirmed published reports, upon his return to St. Louis, that he had brought down about 10,000 pounds. Perhaps it would be more correct to state that he did not deny them.

in the bank, but he wouldn't need to use it to finance sub-
sequent expeditions. Once again he could enjoy virtually
unlimited credit, if he chose to make use of it.

The best estimate of the value of the furs Ashley
brought to St. Louis—at least, the only one that is supported by any sort of documentary evidence—is approximately $50,000. A pack of beaver usually weighed be-
tween ninety and a hundred pounds. One report to the
American Fur Company at the time said that Ashley had
brought back 9,700 pounds of beaver skins. Inasmuch
as they were fine Rocky Mountain skins—these incomparable pelts would soon be known as "Ashley beaver"
in the trade—he undoubtedly received at least $5 a pound
for them.

Ashley himself made only one more trip to the mountains, in 1826. The rendezvous for that year was held
in the Cache Valley, north of the Great Salt Lake. During this journey Ashley sold out to three of his able
lieutenants, Smith, Jackson and Sublette. The transaction
did not mean that he would no longer engage in the fur
trade, however. It meant simply that he was retiring from
the strenuous life in the mountains. His agreement with
the firm of Smith, Jackson and Sublette provided that
he would furnish them with goods and dispose of their
furs in St. Louis as long as they continued in business.
They, too, would operate with the rendezvous system,
and he would send merchandise out to them each summer, and bring back the furs taken during the previous
fall, winter and spring. It was a profitable business.

In his short but distinguished career in the mountains
Ashley brought down to St. Louis more than five hundred packs of beaver, worth in excess of a quarter of a

million dollars. He continued to make a large income from supplying trappers – most of whom had been young men who answered his advertisements – and buying their furs.

When he left his St. Louis mansion to go to Congress in 1831, he was, except for Senator Benton, not only the most influential and distinguished person in the state of Missouri, but one of the richest.

1834

TURNING NUMBER SIX

Crossroads

Private forts, built at strategic locations
in the mountains, supersede the rendezvous,
serve the western fur trade the year round,
and become supply, repair and trading
centers of a new economic era—
The era of mass migration

VI

Crossroads

The Indians come no more to the post,
their travois laden with buffalo robes.
Packs of furs are never launched in bullboats
on the Platte. . . The dust of the Great
White Medicine Road rests beneath a black
velvet boulevard. . . Fort Laramie is
only a shell, but like a sea-born shell, it
still resounds with the music and the voices
that nurtured it. In the high Wyoming winds,
it whistles and moans with the throb
of Sioux tom-toms and the ghost-like
music of forgotten fifes and drums.
    from Hafen and Young's *Fort Laramie*

On a high buffalo grass plain that washed in rough waves against the dark timbered ridges to the west, the Laramie River, swift and clear, came out of the southwest to meet the wide and shallower waters of the North Platte. There, at that unspectacular confluence, for more centuries than may be counted with certainty, was the most important crossroads of the Far West.

If a detailed and accurate map of the region had been obtainable in the year 1834 – which it was not – it would have told an exciting story, yet it would have portrayed little that had not existed there since the day of Creation. The exceptions would have been a very few manmade objects and conditions.

One would have needed to look in no less than half a dozen directions to see the whole picture. The trails one would have seen, flying as an eagle, would be old in the way of the land itself, for they would have been made by the first animals, seeking out their feeding grounds and their havens of safety and their watering holes.

Following a course slightly east of south from this meeting of waters one would have found Crow Creek and the South Platte, and from that stream – depending upon one's purpose – one might have traveled up Box Elder or Kiowa or Bijou creeks, crossed the Platte-Arkansas divide and come upon Fountain or Black Squirrel or Big Sandy Creeks and reached the Arkansas River. All the way – by airline some four hundred miles and much longer by the route a land traveler would be obliged to take – the great wall of the Rockies would stand before the West, throwing long afternoon shadows over the tortured land at their feet. All the way, eastward high arid plains, etched with umber and ochre and glistening white washes would reach to an horizon that was always indefinite in the haze of illimitable distance.

On such a journey one might have seen perhaps two or three marks made by white men: small log, earth or rock shelters with pole corrals beside them which had been erected by itinerant fur hunters, each squalid structure standing alone in the immensity and more than likely occupied by a family of badgers no longer alarmed by the lingering odors of intruders who had vanished as mysteriously as they had come. Occasionally one might have sighted a cluster of skin lodges and the smoke of cooking fires spiraling upward in the sharp clean air, or a war party traveling to or from some foray, moving with caution and swiftness by devious trails to escape detection.

Going on down the Arkansas one would have come upon an important and brand new addition to the imaginary map. Just beyond the Purgatoire the high adobe walls and bastions of Bent's Fort would lift their mud grayness against the dazzling light of the river meadows and bottomlands. An American flag signalling United States territory would whip the breeze above a lookout.

The ruts and ribbons of beaten earth which flowed in from the east were the mountain branch of the Santa Fe Trail, and they twisted and curved on from Bent's Fort a few miles and then crossed the river, fading into the southwest amid the mounting mesas and ridges and the sweeps of pinion. Ahead, beyond Raton Pass, were the routes to Taos and Santa Fe, the foreign soil of Spanish country.

In the summer of 1834, an observer might have seen a hundred and twenty-five wagons, creaking under their heavy loads, rolling over the Cimarron cut-off and the mountain branch, and he would have seen them going back to Independence in the fall, perhaps as many as two hundred men guarding them – a military escort, drivers, scouts, trappers and traders. Bales of hides and furs had supplanted the outbound dry goods and hardwares, and money pouches were heavy with gold and silver specie, returns of some $200,000 in value.

This was a world very different from that north of the Arkansas. Here was an established traffic, a way of life, and a prospering trading house, an organized business with brigades of armed plainsmen conducting it not alone in defiance of the forces of the wilderness, the

burning deserts and rugged terrain, but in defiance of
red raiders who never ceased their attempts to loot the
caravans, to steal the horses and mules, burn the wagons
and kill the defenders.

Turning back to the north one would have found stillness and emptiness, a completely different picture. Looking east from the Laramie's mouth another trail would
have been seen, but the travelers on it would have had
different purposes in mind, different goals, different ob-
jectives from those going to Santa Fe. The packtrains
would be bringing goods, but they would be goods for
the trappers in the mountains, at the annual rendezvous,
wherever it was to be held. There was only one kind
of commerce on this trail, the commerce of the fur trade.

This was the fur trade trail that came out of Westport
Landing, pointed northwest across the Kansas, the Vermilion, the Blue, and turned up the Platte. The branch
from the Council Bluffs ran along the north side of the
river, and they both continued on, one on each bank,
until the mouth of the Laramie had been passed, and
then they became one trail, running up the valley of the
North Platte, on to the Sweetwater and over the great
smooth hump of the South Pass, on and on into vast
regions that only the Mountain Men had penetrated. It
would be called the Oregon Trail, but in the year 1834,
there were no way stations, no forts, no garrisons of soldiers, as there were on that other trail, five hundred miles
to the south. There was nothing on the trail that passed
the Laramie.

Look toward the northwest now. The North Platte
opened the way for more than a hundred miles, but then
one would have been obliged to turn away from it and

traverse the barren benchlands, and a tossing sea of gray and yellow hills. Beyond would be the headwaters of the Powder, and if one skirted the Rattlesnake Range, one would find Badwater and Poison creeks, and they would lead to the Big Horn.

These rivers, one on each side of the Bighorn Mountains, knew a common destiny – the Yellowstone. There would be posts on it, for the keelboats could reach it by way of the great river highway of the West, the Missouri system, and that was the way the Mountain Men had gone from the beginning of the fur trade. However, in all the distance from the Laramie to the Yellowstone – five or six hundred miles, depending upon the trail followed – one would have found no permanent fort. It would have been the same as it was to the south, between the Laramie and the Purgatoire – emptiness and stillness and great blue and white mountains and high dry plateaus and colored gashes through which the streams ran between networks of shimmering cottonwoods.

Look over the compass a little east of north, and it would have been the same, the same for hundreds of miles. Look a little farther to the northeast and a trace would be found, a thread of plains trail which began where Bad River emptied into the Missouri, where Fort Pierre stood, and was woven across the grass sea to the Black Hills, threaded through and around them, and ran on across the Cheyenne and the Niobrara to the North Platte and the Laramie.

Look in any direction from that confluence and there were the countless miles without a permanent habitation, with no system of economics, no established commerce, but that did not mean there was nothing. Far from it.

There were a great many things of meaning, things of importance, things that had existed since the coming of flesh on that earth.

There were the great game herds. There were the oceans of rich grasses on which they lived. There were the storms, the rains and the winds, the drouths and the floods, the burning suns and the snows – all creating a way of natural life. Moving the eyes in an arc, south to east to north, from the Laramie and the Platte one would never fail to see red peoples – the Arapahoe, Cheyenne, Pawnee, Crow, Sioux – always moving like kings and queens and knaves and pawns and knights across the gigantic chessboard that was their realm on earth. They were on the trails long before the first Mountain Men pushed their way down from the Big Horn, up from the Arkansas or out the North Platte.

From every direction the trails crossed where the Laramie reached its end, giving its cold mountain waters to the greater streams that carried them to a far-off sea. The animals grazed there, and the Indians came to hunt them there, to rest there. Following the same ancient trails, the traders stopped there, and guns and pots and lead and bright beads and worthless medals and denim and calicoes and blankets were exchanged for beaver and otter and goat and deer and buffalo and bear skins.

It was the crossroads of time and antiquity, the meeting of wilderness roads, that the forces of the universe through countless ages had carved and delineated, paths that had awaited the coming of the peoples in the universal scheme.

There were five sons in the Sublette family of Kentucky. William was nineteen when they crossed the Mississippi and went on through St. Louis to live in St. Charles. He was twenty-three when he became an Ashley recruit. At twenty-seven he was a partner of Smith, Jackson and Sublette, the new firm to which Ashley sold out. After a prosperous four years, they took a leaf out of the General's book, and in 1830 sold out themselves to another new organization, the Rocky Mountain Fur Company.

The Santa Fe trade next attracted the partners. They started in the spring of 1831 with a fine outfit, twenty wagons and eighty men, and the future appeared brighter than ever before. On the Cimarron, lurking Comanches riddled Jed Smith with arrows. The association was dissolved when Sublette and Jackson returned to St. Louis.

Sublette, unattached and fancy free, with a substantial bank account, took a pack train of his own out to the trappers' rendezvous in Pierre's Hole in the summer of 1832. That was the scene of the great fight with the Blackfeet. He fought beside his old friend, Robert Campbell, with whom he had shared so many perils during the past decade in the mountains. They made oral wills to each other, but they lived through the terrible day, and went back to St. Louis with their bond of friendship made stronger by the experience.

Like the leader he had served loyally and had so greatly admired, Sublette would succumb to political ambitions. He would run for Congress, and his supporters would cry of him: "Pioneer of the Far West. His experience, fit age, chivalric character, his intimate acquaintance with the people, and their confidence in him, and above all his undeviating adherence to, and practice of, the pure Democratic-Republican principles through his past life, are the qualifications which endear him to the people." Not enough people held the same opinion, however, and he was defeated.

It didn't matter. He was well-to-do. But he wasn't an idler. In 1841 he would become an aide-de-camp to Governor Thomas Reynolds of Missouri. Four years later he would be on his way to Washington to confer with Senator Benton about an appointment as Superintendent of Indian Affairs in St. Louis. He would have been a good man for the post. The Indians were his friends, his brothers. Throughout all the Indian country, the warriors spoke of him by the name of Fate.

He didn't talk with the senator. Death intervened.

In 1824, when Robert Campbell reached St. Louis from his birthplace in County Tyrone, Ireland, he was twenty years old. A few months later his death appeared imminent. He was stricken with lung hemorrhages. His physician thought a drier climate might be beneficial to him, and concealing the nature of his illness he secured a place on the famous Ashley expedition of 1825. The complete restoration of his health came quickly in the mountains. He became a Mountain Man, and his exceptional intellect combined with his unqualified physical courage soon brought him to positions of leadership and responsibility.

Campbell gave up the rigorous mountain life in 1835, but not his interest in the fur trade. He would be a trader for years, and as a businessman of great talent, he would become the president of two banks and the owner of a hotel. Because of his exceptional knowledge of Indian affairs, and his profound understanding of them, Washington would repeatedly seek his services in treaty negotions. He would be with Father de Smet at the great council held near Fort Laramie in 1851, and President Grant would send him on similar missions.

The young man who had lung hemorrhages would live to be seventy-five, dying in St. Louis in 1879, wealthy, honored and respected by all who had associated with him.

When Sublette and Campbell returned to St. Louis in the fall of 1832 from the rendezvous in Pierre's Hole, they were contemplating a daring scheme. They put their heads together and by December had agreed upon a course. They formed a partnership with the sole purpose of opposing the Astor monopoly on the upper Missouri River.

If the plan appeared inconceivable to men of less courage and ambition, it did not appear in that light to Sublette and Campbell. They were convinced that they stood on solid ground. The venture they proposed to carry out had not evolved from whims or dreams, and, in all justice, it must be considered as illustrating their remarkable understanding of the conditions of the time, their astonishing perspicacity, and their extraordinary business acumen.

The rendezvous had made one thing forcefully apparent: the mountains were becoming overcrowded. The competition was not only dishonorable and disgraceful but was rapidly becoming ruinous. Keeping this indisputable fact in mind, Sublette and Campbell gave their serious attention to another situation, one which, if less

alarming, was exceedingly interesting in the questions
it presented.

More than two years before ,a strong rumor had swept
through the fur trade that Astor would soon retire. If
many of his competitors prayed that the rumor was true,
Astor's chief lieutenants did not believe him. Robert
Stuart, head of the Northern Department of the American
Fur Company,[1] had written a trader: "Pray, give your-
self no concern about Mr. Astor's retiring   .   .   .   my
opinion is that he will never retire *until he is called. . .*"
Ramsay Crooks, general manager of the immense Western Department,[2] held a similar view, and told his associate, Pierre Chouteau, that to Astor the business was "like
an only child and he cannot muster courage to part with
it."

Both Stuart and Crooks were indulging in wishful
thinking. They understood fully the effect that Astor's
withdrawal would have on the international fur trade.
Fully as astute as the Astor managers, fully as conversant with conditions, Sublette and Campbell could readily realize the changes which would inevitably take place
in the trade with the departure from it of the man who
had for so many years dominated it.

How much Sublette and Campbell really knew of
Astor's feelings and intentions cannot be determined –
it is hardly conceivable that they had access to his letters – and, therefore, it is doubtful they were apprised
that at the very time they were scheming to oppose him
he had already made up his mind to close his doors in
the year 1833. Moreover, they had forgotten – if, indeed,

---

[1] Michigan, Wisconsin, Minnesota, Illinois, Indiana, and Ohio.
[2] The Missouri River, Great Plains, and Rocky Mountains.

they ever knew it—that 1833 was the year in which the charter of the American Fur Company would expire. It had been granted by the New York state legislature in 1808 for a period of twenty-five years. Had they known that, they would have reasoned that a drastic change, perhaps a complete reorganization of the company, most certainly would take place. In all probability they would have postponed decisive action until they had learned the nature of the change.

The truth seems to be that Sublette and Campbell proposed to fight Astor in the unqualified belief they could benefit. Other St. Louis traders, getting wind of their plan, shook their heads in dismay and joined in the view that they were being driven into a foolhardy venture by sheer bravado and unmitigated egotism. No one had ever beaten Astor in a trade war, and the general conviction was that it could not be done.

It was not courage and ego that motivated Sublette and Campbell as much as it was certain conditions which inspired supreme confidence in them.

When they had announced the formation of their partnership in December 1832, General Ashley—now Congressman Ashley—had taken the floor of the House to endorse the enterprise of his two talented proteges, to praise them as men of commendable character and exceptional ability, and to predict great success for them. These accolades gave rise to the rumor that Ashley himself was planning to reenter the fur trade and was a silent partner in the new firm. Several bankers and supply houses promptly made Sublette and Campbell generous offers of loans and credit. This turn of events was not only duly noted and studied by Astor, in Europe, and Crooks, in St. Louis, but it brought about a change in the attitude of all traders. The previous predictions of disaster for Sublette and Campbell were qualified with the admission that perhaps these two brash young Mountain Men would, after all, be powerful enough to give old Astor a run for his money.

In the end, however, it wouldn't be Astor who would be directly under their attack. It would be his snobbish, cold son, William Backhouse Astor, in New York, and his two lieutenants, Crooks and Chouteau, in St. Louis, in all of whom he was obliged to place his trust. Could Astor have remained in command through the year 1833, the story of Sublette and Campbell would have had a tragic ending, but Astor would not be in a position to keep a firm hand on the helm.

Astor would be seriously ill in Europe. He had gone there in June 1832. July 17th was his seventieth birthday, but he had little reason to celebrate. What he saw ahead of him was unpleasant for him to contemplate. He saw a long hill down which the profits in the fur trade would steadily descend from the great height they had reached, and he had determined that he would not march down that hill with them. A sinister new force would rise to further injure fur markets already dangerously depressed. "I very much fear," Astor would write Chouteau, "Beaver will not sell very well soon unless very fine, it appears they make *hats of silk in place of Beaver.*"

He would not be able to return home in the fall of 1832, as he had planned. A fall from his bed would augment his afflictions by shocking his nerves. "I think now," he would tell his aides, "to Remain in Europe till Spring in Deed I am not able to go back & in winter I Do not wish to."

The passing months would bring more distress and sadness. His daughter, Eliza, and her husband, Viscount Vincent Rumpff, would be stricken by cholera and would narrowly escape death. His sister, Elizabeth, and two of his grandchildren, also would be victims of the terrible plague then raging throughout most of the world. His brother, Henry, would die.

At the very time when Sublette and Campbell would be starting their drive, in the spring of 1833, Astor, his health but little improved, would not be taking a ship for New York. He would be retreating from Paris to his villa at Lake Geneva. There his doctors would struggle to prevent his complete collapse.

There, too, he would take the action that would be a gravestone for the American Fur Company as he had created it. In July 1833, he would send a formal announcement to Bernard Pratte and Company, his agents in St. Louis. "Wishing to retire from the Concern in which I am angaged with your House," he would write, "you will please to take this as notice thereof, & that the agreement entered into on the 7th May 1830 – between your House & me . . . will expire with the outfit of the present year on the terms expressed in said agreement."

That would mean that some time in the winter of 1833-1834, after all furs collected during the previous spring, summer and fall had been brought into St. Louis and sold, the greatest fur trader of all history would close his doors.

It would be too late to stop Sublette and Campbell. Their offensive would have been underway for a year. While Astor would be fighting for life, a transaction which he would never have permitted would be consummated without his knowledge, on the Missouri four thousand miles from the luxurious garden in which he was a helpless prisoner.

In the spring of 1833, Sublette and Campbell moved with the precision and efficiency of a well trained military force.

Campbell started with a caravan from Westport[3] in April for the annual midsummer rendezvous, which would be held on upper Green River. He took the route up the Platte, the Sweetwater and across South Pass, reaching his destination without serious difficulties.

The rendezvous was boisterous, drunken, carnal — and important. It made forcefully apparent the chaotic condition into which the mountain fur trade had been driven by competition. In addition to Campbell's caravan, brigades were there from the Rocky Mountain Fur Company, the Upper Missouri Outfit of the American Fur Company, parties led by Nathaniel Wyeth and Benjamin Louis Eulalie de Bonneville, bands from several small companies, and numerous free trappers. Altogether more than three hundred white men were present who had been taking furs during the previous spring.[4] The result was that any profits made were inconsequential, hardly more than enough to meet expenses, and the books of some brigades showed an increase in red ink entries. An

---

[3] Kansas City.

[4] It is perhaps irrelevant to mention that the rendezvous was attended also by several score warriors and the usual number of enterprising squaws taking advantage of the opportunity they enjoyed only once a year to sell their charms at outrageous prices. Their presence had nothing to do with the deterioration of the fur trade.

exception was the firm of Sublette and Campbell. The merchandise and equipment Robert Campbell brought out was sold (a large part on credit, of course) at no less than a two hundred per cent markup, and some articles brought an even greater return. He had furs valued at more than $30,000 in his possession when he left the rendezvous.

Carrying out a prearranged plan to meet William Sublette at the mouth of the Yellowstone, Campbell took a pack train back over South Pass, turned off the Sweetwater on a mountain trail to Beaver Creek and going down it reached the Big Horn, a short distance above its junction with Wind River. Traveling with Campbell were Milton Sublette, his partner's younger brother, and Thomas Fitzpatrick, the veteran Mountain Man whom the Indians called Broken Hand, both members of the Rocky Mountain Fur Company; Nathaniel Wyeth, and several British sportsmen.

Shortly before reaching the Little Big Horn, Fitzpatrick and his men, accompanied by the Britishers, left for Tongue River. It was Fitzpatrick's intention to make a fall hunt in the Crow country. Before he started, however, he and Milton Sublette, as representatives of the Rocky Mountain Fur Company, formulated an agreement with Wyeth to purchase $3,000 worth of merchandise which Wyeth would bring out to the rendezvous of 1834.

The Big Horn being navigable at this point, the others constructed bull boats and traveled in them to the mouth of the Yellowstone. Sublette had not arrived, and Campbell established a camp to wait for him. Wyeth continued on down the Missouri, passing the keelboat in which

Sublette was ascending the river a few hours after leaving Fort Union, the headquarters of the American Fur Company's Upper Missouri Outfit at the confluence of the Yellowstone and Missouri rivers.

Soon after Campbell had set out with the caravan for the mountains in April 1833, William Sublette was traveling up the Missouri in the steamboat *Otto* with an immense cargo of equipment, merchandise and supplies. Fighting its way up the perilous spring flood of the great river, the *Otto* made intentional stops in the vicinity of each major American Fur Company post. At these landings, Sublette left groups of men, well supplied with tools and trade goods, to establish rival posts.

At Fort Pierre[5] the remaining cargo was transferred to keelboats. The *Otto* turned back downstream, and Sublette and his men went on by pole and cordelle power. It was his plan to erect a competing post near Fort Pierre later in the fall.[6] En route to meet Campbell at the Yellowstone, Sublette built only one other post above Fort Pierre — near the Mandan Villages, to compete with the Upper Missouri Outfit's post there.

On August 28th, 1833, Sublette came into sight of Fort Union and Campbell's camp. The two prongs of the attack had come together.

The headquarters of the Upper Missouri Outfit, Fort Union, was the largest, strongest and finest post on the Missouri. Indeed, in the entire West only Bent's Fort on the Arkansas could be compared with it. In command was the dynamic, shrewd, unscrupulous and colorful

---

[5] Pierre, South Dakota.
[6] It was built by Sublette and Campbell men in October 1833.

Kenneth McKenzie. He ruled over his immense domain in the manner of a feudal lord, maintained military discipline, lived like a wealthy country squire, and sometimes wore plumes in his hat and a coat of chain mail.

Sublette and Campbell had been united only a day before they began to build the post which would defy the monopoly enjoyed by McKenzie. They selected a site opposite the Yellowstone's mouth, three miles by land and six miles by water below Fort Union. Sublette remained only long enough to see the work well underway – the post would be christened Fort William in his honor – then with his brother, Milton, and a complement of *voyageurs* set off in a keelboat for St. Louis, taking the furs Campbell had brought from the rendezvous. Campbell remained to command the post and direct the company's fall hunt.

The attitude of Kenneth McKenzie, on whom fell the full responsibility of combatting the onslaught of Sublette and Campbell, is best disclosed in a letter he wrote to his lieutenant, D. D. Mitchell, who was stationed at Fort McKenzie, an Upper Missouri Outfit post in the Blackfoot country. The letter also gives an accounting of events which took place up to January 21, 1834, although not with the accuracy that would be greatly appreciated. However, McKenzie was not one to put himself in a bad light, the truth notwithstanding. McKenzie told Mitchell:

> Sublette and Campbell arrived here August 29th, and soon fixed on a site for their fort which they have built two miles below me and called Fort William. They came up with a great force with a very large outfit and abundance of alcohol and wines highly charged with spirits. They engaged the

three young Deschamps as interpreters at salaries of $500 per annum each, and Tom Kipland at $600.[7] They had, moreover, a full complement of clerks and seemed prepared to carry all before them, nothing doubting but that they would secure at least one half the trade of the country. They abandoned the idea of sending to the Blackfeet this season. They started a small equipment on horses to the Crow village on Wind river. They were expected to return early in December but have not yet been heard of. . . although on their first start here they made great show and grand promise to the Indians and although among the men nothing was talked about but the new company, they live now at the sign of 'The case is altered.' Their interpreters have quarreled and left them, and are now working hard for me. The Indians find their promises mere empty words. . . They have a post near to Riviere au Tremble[8] in opposition to Chardon where they are doing literally nothing. Chardon has it all his own way. They have another post on the Yellowstone[9] in opposition to Pillot and Brazeau and there they get no robes although they offer a blanket of scarlet for a robe.

McKenzie had not hesitated to take the offensive. The idea that he might be defeated was inconceivable to him. Astor's depthless resources were available, and no one with less money and manpower could successfully defy the *company*.

He was right, of course, but there were elements in the picture he could not see, forces that he could not

---

[7] Unusually high salaries.

[8] Riviere aux Trembles, or Poplar River. The Upper Missouri Outfit post there was Fort Jackson, built in December 1833, with C. A. Chardon in command, for the express purpose, as stated by McKenzie, of compelling his new opponents, Sublette and Campbell, "to divide their forces, for the principle of divide and conquer has often been verified."

[9] Braseau's Houses stood on the left bank of the Yellowstone some fifty miles above its mouth. However, whether this is the post to which McKenzie referred is not ascertainable.

have been expected to anticipate, as he sent orders to the Upper Missouri Outfit's posts to drive the upstarts out at all costs. His letter to Mitchell continued:

> You must be aware that I have not been asleep this fall. It has cost me something to secure the Indians to me, but being determined to get the peltries, nothing has been neglected that would carry my point. My opponents cannot by any means get peltries sufficient to pay the wages of their men. At the Gros Ventres and the Mandans they have not even robes to sleep on. At the Mandans my last account states that Picotte[10] has eighty packs of robes and five hundred beaver, the opposition two packs of robes and eight beaver, and I hope things are equally promising lower down.
>
> . . . Mr. Campbell called on me . . . and proposed to sell out to me all their interest on the river. I listened to his terms, but was by no means disposed to buy out the opposition, when all my old experienced and faithful clerks and tradesmen felt so certain of driving them out; especially on my giving them *carte blanche* with respect to trade at their respective posts, of course to be used with discretion but with this condition, that all peltries must be secured for the A. F. Co. and thus far I have no reason to complain. The new company is now in bad odor and must sink.

McKenzie was the law on the upper river – at least, he considered himself so. He operated a still at Fort Union, producing whiskey that was quite palatable, and dispensing it openly in his transactions with Indians.[11]

---

[10] Honore Picotte, formerly with the Columbia Fur Company and the French Fur Company. He served with the Upper Missouri Outfit for twenty years.

[11] Federal law forbade the transporting of liquor of any kind in the Indian country or its use in the trade. Rigid inspections were being made of all cargoes moving up the Missouri River, and large shipments of alcohol had been confiscated.

He frankly admitted in a dispatch to his superior, Chouteau, at St. Louis that his agents had induced some Crows to rob Fitzpatrick of horses, furs and equipment. It was a severe blow to the Rocky Mountain Fur Company, for Fitzpatrick was prevented from conducting a hunt in the Crow country as he had planned.

The *carte blanche* McKenzie had given his traders in the fight against Sublette and Campbell was exactly that. They were free to pay any price, to be as prodigal with alcohol as they wished, in keeping the intruders from obtaining furs. The method was costly and wiped out all profits, but it was effective. At the Mandans, for example, as much as $12 was paid for a single beaver skin worth no more than $2. Sublette and Campbell could not stand up under such pressure. If it continued much longer they would be driven from the field.

McKenzie's boast that he was winning the fight would be substantiated by good authority, one of Sublette and Campbell's best traders. He was the noted Mountain Man, Charles Larpenteur, who was with Campbell at Fort William. "The Indians had no confidence in his [Campbell's] remaining," he would write, "so that the bulk of the trade went to the American Fur Company in spite of all we could do. . . This post was not the only one that was out of luck, for all those along the Missouri proved a failure."

McKenzie was winning, but the strong forces of which he was unaware were coming closer.

On his way to St. Louis from Fort Union in the fall of 1832, Nathaniel Wyeth had stopped in Fort Leavenworth and reported to government authorities that McKenzie was operating a still. The intelligence was promptly relayed to the Indian Department. William Sublette, profoundly worried by the discouraging outlook, jumped at the opportunity to bring the matter to the attention of Congressman Ashley. Howls were soon heard from the many enemies of the American Fur Company in both Washington and St. Louis.

Shortly thereafter came a charge from Fitzpatrick that he had been robbed – even his own watch had been taken – by agents of the American Fur Company. More howls of protest resounded in Congress when Ashley disseminated this information with appropriate denunciations of unconscionable Astor monopoly. Sublette added his own strong voice to the tumult.

Alarmed, Chouteau quickly got off an express to McKenzie advising him of the menacing situation, and adding: "The dragoons will perhaps be ordered to make a tour along the base of the mountains, and in that case it is possible that they will pay you a visit. You will therefore prepare for their reception and especially for any *searches* which they may make. . ."

Chouteau was telling McKenzie to hide all incriminating evidence.

McKenzie scoffed. He was king of the Upper Missouri and the mountains. His power was insuperable, and that fact was being demonstrated at the moment. He had Sublette and Campbell on the run. He had them beaten. They could not survive through the season.

The dragoons didn't come, but another express did. McKenzie was staggered by its message. In the absence of his father, William Backhouse Astor had approved an agreement, which had been proposed by Ramsay Crooks and Pierre Chouteau, under which the firm of Sublette and Campbell would be purchased by the American Fur Company.

Sublette obviously had made an extremely advantageous deal, for he also had won from Astor a concession of major importance: the American Fur Company would not participate in the mountain trade during the 1834 season.

It was a bitter pill for McKenzie to swallow, and he cursed Crooks and Chouteau as weaklings who had lost, not only their courage but the business ability with which he had credited them. The truth was that in the face of the mounting antagonism emanating from Washington, and the fear that, through General Ashley's influence, Sublette and Campbell might well obtain credit that would let them carry on the fight for at least another year—during which McKenzie would be forced to continue the practice of paying exorbitant prices for furs—Crooks and Chouteau had concluded that the wisest and most beneficial course would be to eliminate Sublette and Campbell by buying them out.

Their thinking was explained by Chouteau in his letter to McKenzie. He wrote:

> By the enclosed agreement, you will see that we have concluded an arrangement at New York with Mr. Sublette. We take such of his equipment in merchandise, utensils, etc., as remains at the close of the season's trade[12] and we retire from the mountain trade for the ensuing year. . . In making this arrangement our object was to keep Sublette from purchasing new equipment and from connecting himself with houses that were making him all sorts of offers. His reputation and that of his patron, Ashley, whatever may be the cause, are far above this worth. Nevertheless, such is the fact

---

[12] January 1, 1834.

and it is enough to procure them unlimited credit. It is this
which induced us to offer to buy them out. We hope,
therefore, that, taking all things into consideration you will
approve of the transaction.

McKenzie took the last sentence as a gross personal
insult, but he could do nothing but accept the situation.
He stood muttering his epithets as the keelboats of Sublette and Campbell vanished down the river.

The most valuable asset that Sublette and Campbell
possessed in the winter of 1833-1834 was not the money
they had received for the equipment and merchandise
at their Missouri River posts, not their good credit, but
the withdrawal of the American Fur Company from
the mountain trade for a year.[13] McKenzie would be prevented from sending a supply caravan to the annual rendezvous. This was an achievement for which they had
not dared to hope – if they had thought of it at all – when
they had launched their fight against the Astor colossus.
They wasted no time, however, patting themselves of the
back.

In their planning, they quickly settled upon two courses
of action.

ONE: They would enlarge their trading store in St.
Louis, increase inventories, and make a drive to capture
a large part of the business of furnishing traders with
goods and supplies. This would throw them directly into
competition with Pratte, Chouteau and Company, but
the agreement under which they had sold out did not

---

[13] Pratte, Chouteau & Company purchased Astor's Western Department
when he retired. Although the name American Fur Company continued
in use for many years, the corporation was legally dead.

preclude them from entering this field. It had said nothing to prevent them from competing with Astor's successors, nor with anyone else, for that matter, as St. Louis merchandisers.[14]

TWO: They would themselves take a caravan to the 1834 rendezvous in the mountains. Competition in this enterprise would come from Wyeth, but that was not a situation which gave them great concern, although they were aware that Wyeth's own plans had been greatly expanded during the winter. He had an agreement to take out $3,000 worth of supplies for the Rocky Mountain Fur Company, and this, although a comparatively small amount, served him as a *point d'appui* which he utilized as a means of securing substantial financial support in Boston. He organized the Columbia River Fishing and Trading Company, picturing in vivid colors his grandiose plans. He sent a supply ship, the *May Dacre,* from Boston in January 1834, bound for the Columbia River, and hurried to St. Louis to prepare his overland caravan. His head was filled with the dream of securing the bulk of the mountain trade as well as that of the Columbia basin.

Sublette and Campbell saw the matter in an entirely different light. Energetic, capable and determined as Wyeth was, they felt confident that he could be outmaneuvered, and that old friendships and loyalties among the Mountain Men, especially those of the Rocky Mountain Fur Company—such former associates as Thomas Fitzpatrick, James Bridger and Henry Fraeb, for example —would give them an advantage. Moreover, they saw

---

[14] The Sublette and Campbell store in St. Louis was highly successful, and they even sold goods to posts of the American Fur Company.

themselves in the position of being able to undersell
Wyeth, who must make a return to his backers. They
could absorb losses he could not.

One may well wonder exactly what event or condition or expressed view or uttered or printed words first
brought Sublette and Campbell to the consideration of
their third course. It seems unlikely that a single force
was responsible for turning them to it. The assumption
that appears most logical is that it, too, evolved out of
a combination of circumstances. They were astute businessmen. They had a thorough understanding of the
economics of the fur trade. They knew well the conditions then existing in the mountains. Even more important, they were fully cognizant of events taking place
in the Mississippi Valley and adjacent country, and their
perspicacity was great enough to alert them to the shadows of forthcoming changes.

They needed no map to guide them on the third course.
All they needed to do was to project their thoughts out
to the mountains, that immense empty region through
which they had wandered for more than a decade, the
trails of which they knew so well, to know what they
would do in that spring of 1834.

Wyeth had been smart enough to purchase most of
his trade goods in Boston, but when he reached St. Louis
with them he found the town ready to take advantage
of him in every other possible way. He wrote his spon-
sors that his opposition had made him "pay a heavy
advance on men and high prices for horses. . . everything
is favorable except that the expense will be greater than
has been calculated." With a company of seventy men

he started his train out of Independence on April 28, 1834, gratified that the Sublette and Campbell caravan had not yet gone.[15]

Milton Sublette, intending to conduct a fall trapping expedition after the rendezvous, had started with the train, but ten days out a diseased leg forced him to turn back. He had not traveled far on his return trip when he met the caravan of his brother and Campbell.

Sublette and Campbell, having been delayed beyond the time scheduled for their departure, were pushing their twenty wagons ahead at record speed. They came up with Wyeth's train on May 12th, rejected a suggestion that the two companies travel together, and pressed on. Wyeth quickly prepared a letter to Fitzpatrick, advising him that he was en route with the goods for which the Rocky Mountain Fur Company had contracted, and Sublette agreed to deliver it. As he watched Sublette and Campbell's wagons disappear into the western sky, Wyeth's concern mounted. Had Milton Sublette, whom he considered an honorable man, been able to complete the trip, he might have been less apprehensive. He had little faith, however, in Fitzpatrick, and perhaps even less in William Sublette. He was plagued by the unpleasant suspicion that with both himself and Milton absent when Sublette and Campbell arrived at the rendezvous any thought of honoring his contract would be negligible if not completely accidental. All he could do was push on as fast as he could, and hope for the best.

---

[15] Also traveling with the Wyeth caravan were Jason and Daniel Lee, the first misionaries to cross the country, Thomas Nuttall, curator of Harvard University Botanical Garden, and John Townsend, a young ornithologist from Philadelphia.

Sublette and Campbell, indeed, had traveled fast. Wyeth was four days behind them when he reached the Laramie River on June 1. There he saw a sight which not only startled him, but gave him reason to dwell upon profound considerations.

As intelligent as he was enterprising, Wyeth realized that he was a witness to an event of transcending importance. Campbell had gone on to the rendezvous, but a large part of the caravan had been left on the Laramie, and there Sublette with thirteen men had begun to build a fort of extensive proportions. As he went on with his own train up the North Platte, Wyeth could well realize that a new and significant era had begun in the western fur trade.

Perhaps Sublette and Campbell had not been ahead of all the others in their thinking. There were many men in the fur trade with shrewd, analytical minds, and they could realize the meaning of events taking place, understand conditions, detect a trend, as well as anyone. The difference was that Sublette and Campbell took action, did something about it, while the others were still musing on the situation.

The picture was not mysterious. It was drawn in simple lines, with great clarity. Eleven points would explain it.

1 – The rendezvous system had been adequate as long as white men did the trapping, and beaver was the chief article of the trade.

2 – The quantity of beaver was rapidly diminishing, however, while the number of trappers increased. Skins were smaller, for young animals were being taken. It

was swiftly becoming more difficult for any company to make a worthwhile profit.

3 – Substitutes were beginning to supplant fur for hats. Well-dressed men were turning to cloth and silk.

4 – The market for buffalo robes was steadily increasing. They were finding growing favor as coats, carriage robes, and even floor coverings.

5 – Indians lived with and from the buffalo. They procured them in large numbers for food and clothing and lodges, and, even more important to the trader, they treated and preserved and tanned them into beautiful soft skins and robes. White men possessed no such skills, nor would they attempt to compete with the Indians. Tanning buffalo hides was squaw's work.

6 – Beaver skins could be tied into neat packs, weighing no more than a hundred pounds, and easily transported by packhorse or bullboat. Buffalo hides were bulky and heavy. Wagons were needed if a trader was to transport enough of them to make a good return on an expedition.

7 – Buffalo robes were produced by Indians in widely scattered hunting camps – they followed the herds. They wanted to trade them, but unless they could bring them to a permanent post this commerce could not very well be conducted to the advantage of either the producer or the buyer.

8 – The high plains east of the mountains were incredibly rich in game of all kinds – buffalo, deer, antelope, wolves, goats and sheep.

9 – A permanent fort and trading post strategically located at the foot of the mountains would be available

to both the mountain trappers and the Indians. Large stocks of supplies and merchandise could be maintained in safety. There would be storage room for the hides. Wagon caravans from Westport could bring out supplies and return with the furs and hides.

10 – Supply trains still could be sent out to the annual rendezvous if desirable.

11 – A strong fort could be open for trade throughout the year.

Sublette and Campbell knew the place for it, the most strategic place for a fort between the Arkansas and the Yellowstone, the junction of the Laramie and North Platte rivers, where all the trails of the high plains crossed.

They headed for it.[16]

On June 1, Nathaniel Wyeth would write in his journal:

"Made 15 miles to Laramies fork. . . At the crossing we found 13 of Sublettes men camped for the purpose of building a fort he having gone ahead with his best animals and the residue of his goods he left about 14 loads."

And on the same day the missionary Jason Lee would record:

". . . arrived at Laramas Fork and forded it without difficulty before dinner. . . This stream is generally very difficult to cross, it being very rapid. Some

---

[16] Legend has it that a trapper named (Joseph?) Larame, or Laramee, was killed by Indians (or maybe drowned) in the stream in 1821. He has not been otherwise identified, but his name was given not only to a river, but to a mountain range, a high peak, a town, a county, and to the most famous fort in all western history. In the days of Sublette and Campbell, the range immediately to the west of the Laramie River was called by trappers the Black Hills.

of Subletts men who are building a trading-fort a little distance came to us   they are planting corn."

Later, the noted trader, Lucien Fontenelle, would report to Pierre Chouteau that William Sublette had built a fort "on Laramie's Fork of the River Platte and can make it a central place for the Sioux and Cheyenne trade. He has now men running after these Indians to bring them to the River Platte. Buffalo is in abundance on that river during all seasons of the year, and the situation may turn out to be an advantageous one for the trade."

Wyeth would hurry on, burdened with his apprehensions about his own interests and harboring profound thoughts about the fort on the Laramie. Still three days behind William Sublette, he reached the rendezvous, which was held on Ham's Fork of the Green, on June 19th, His worst fears were immediately realized. Sublette had succeeded in inducing the partners of the Rocky Mountain Fur Company to ignore their contract.

Sharp words were exchanged. Wyeth thundered at Fitzpatrick and Sublette that he would "roll a stone into their garden which they would never be able to get out." However, a letter to Milton Sublette said soberly: "I do not accuse you or him (Fitzpatrick) of any intention of injuring me in this manner when you made the contract, but I think he has been bribed to sacrifice my interests by better offers from your brother."

Wyeth was too intelligent and too courageous to remain long in the dumps. Besides, he was burning with a new idea.

He took his train westward — forty-one men, one hundred and twenty-six horses, and all the merchandise he had brought from Boston and St. Louis—and on July 14th reached the Snake River, a little above the mouth of the Portneuf.

Two days later he, too, had begun to build a fort. He would recount the event to a friend in this way:

> Since mine of June 21st from Ham's Fork, I have, as I then proposed, built a fort on Snake or Lewis river in Lat. 43 deg. 14 min. N. and Long. 113 deg. 30 min. w. which I named Fort Hall in honor of the oldest genetleman in the concern. We manufactured a magnificent flag from some unbleached sheeting, a little red flannel and a few blue patches; saluted it with damaged powder and wet it in villanous alcohol. . . [the fort] is manned by twelve men and has constantly loaded in the bastions 100 guns and rifles. These bastions command both the inside and outside.

Wyeth went on to the Columbia. He had made good his threat to Fitzpatrick and Sublette. Fort Hall was the stone he had rolled into their garden—it would take much of the mountain trade, competition they would never succeed in "rolling out."

Meanwhile, a christening also had taken place on the Laramie. Champagne had been used. The name bestowed as the foundation log was laid, was Fort William.

It was the first, and it would have the longest life, but not with the names of Sublette and Campbell above its gate.

Adverse conditions had brought about the dissolution of the Rocky Mountain Fur Company. Thomas Fitzpatrick, Milton Sublette and James Bridger had formed a new partnership. They would continue to operate in the mountains, but their furs would be delivered for disposition to Lucien Fontenelle. The arrangement is historically noteworthy. Fontenelle was affiliated with Pratte, Chouteau and Company. They were the successors of Astor's great Western Department, and they were still popularly known as the American Fur Company.

In the spring of 1835, Sublette and Campbell took out a long supply caravan. Unexpectedly they received an offer from Fitzpatrick, Sublette and Bridger for Fort William. It did not take them long to accept it.

Inasmuch as the buyers would sell their furs and robes entirely through Fontenelle of Pratte, Chouteau and Company, Fort William, it might be said, fell under the control of the American Fur Company.

Astor wasn't there, but his ghost was.

Mountain Men thought more in terms of geography than in given names. It wasn't that they didn't like the name *William,* or that they wished to offend its builder, it was simply that there had been, and were, a number of *Fort Williams.* If you said *Fort Laramie,* no one could

---

[17] More famous and infamous men and women visited Fort Laramie than any other post in the West. It is the scene of literally hundreds of episodes and events related in countless narratives, journals, diaries and commercial and military reports. One interested in learning more of its history would do well to read *Fort Laramie and the Pageant of the West, 1834-90,* by LeRoy R. Hafen and Francis Marion Young, Glendale, Calif., 1938, and if more detail and information are desired, see Chittenden, *History of the American Fur Trade;* Spaulding, ed., *On the Oregon Trail: Robert Stuart's Journey;* Morgan, *West of William Ashley;* Wislizenus, *Journey to the Rocky Mountains;* Dale, *Ashley-Smith Explorations;* Hafen and Ghent, *Broken Hand;* Irving, *Adventures of Bonneville;* Young, ed., *Correspondence and Journals of Wyeth;* C. G. Coutant, *History of Wyoming,* Laramie, 1899; Francis Parkman, *The Oregon Trail,* many editions; Chittenden and Richardson, *Life . . . of de Smet;* Ralph Moody, *The Old Trails West,* New York, 1963; Marvin Ross, *The West of Alfred Jacob Miller,* Norman, Okla., 1951 (paintings). Anyone who reads these books will be an expert on Fort Laramie's early days.

misunderstand your meaning, and everyone knew exactly where it was.

So the name Fort Laramie came into general usage, the name of an obscure man about whom almost nothing is known but who will live forever in history, remembered by a monument which marked a vital turning in the course of the American West.[17]

Index

Abbott, Samuel: 147

Absaroka: 98

Airs, James: 16

American Fur Co: 69, 86, 89, 119, 124, 129, 137, 145, 147, 155, 158-59, 162, 164, 207, 221, 223, 226, 229-33, 242; Upper Missouri Outfit, 118, 126, 154, 163, 226-27, 229; Northern Dept., 144, 149, 153-54, 158, 160, 220; Western Dept., 147, 150, 152, 154-55, 161-63, 220, 242

Arapaho Indians: 216

Arikara Indians: 23-24, 53-55, 73, 97, 150, 190-91, 194-95, 198-99, 206

Ashley, Gen. William H: 148-51, 153, 164, 167-69, 174, 178-81, 183-208, 217-18, 221, 231-32; characteristics, 170; pre-fur-trade ventures, 170-72; narrative of, 191-94, 200-02, 204-05

Assiniboine Indians: 54, 126, 185

Astor, John Jacob: 68-70, 79, 83-91, 96, 101-02, 104, 120-23, 125-26, 130, 137, 139-64, 168, 175, 188, 219-23, 228, 231, 233-34, 242

Astor, William Backhouse: 222, 231-32

Astoria: 79, 90-91, 95, 100-03, 138, 175

Astorians: 16, 79; overland exped., 90, 95-102; exped. by sea, 90-95

Atkinson, Gen. Henry: 205

Bates, Frederick: 50-51

Bear River: 176

Beckwourth, James P: 202, 204

Benton, Sen. Thomas: 208, 218

Bent's Fort: 213, 226

Bernard Pratte & Co: 152, 154-58, 160, 223

Berthold and Chouteau: 142-43, 145, 147

Big Horn River: 54, 57-58, 60, 65-66, 68, 77-78, 197-98, 205

Bighorn Mountains: 24

Big Knife River: 73

Black, Capt: 103

Blackfeet Indians: 56-57, 60-62, 66, 74-75, 97, 126, 149-51, 179, 187-88, 190, 197, 206, 217, 227-28

Blanc, Gros: 50-51, 54-56, 71-73

Blood Indians: 126

Bradbury, John: 62-64, 96

Braseau's Houses: 228

Bridger, James: 183, 200, 202, 234, 241

Burr, Aaron: 40

Cabanne, John: 141-43

Cabanne and Co: 142, 144

Cache Valley: 203-04

Calhoun, John C. (Secy. of War): 180

Campbell, Robert: 202, 217-18, 226-27, 229-30, 237, 239

Carson, Alexander: 79, 97, 99, 202

Carson, Moses: 145

Cass (Astorian): 79, 99

Cauldron Linn: 100
Cedar Island: 77
Chardon, C. A: 228
Cheyenne Indians: 15, 98, 216, 240
Cheyenne River: 156
Chouteau, Auguste: 16, 33, 41, 54, 55
Chouteau, Pierre: 24, 72-73, 118-23, 125, 145, 152, 154-55, 157-58, 160, 164, 220, 222, 230-32, 240
Clark, William: 13-15, 25, 37, 42, 46, 50-51, 53-54, 62, 65-66, 78, 90, 138
Clemson, Capt. Eli B: 72
Clinton, DeWitt: 85-86
Clyman, James: 189, 202; diary of, 190
Collier & Powell (Columbia Fur Co. subsidiary): 153, 157
Colorado River: 25, 26, 206
Colter, John: 15-16, 52-53, 56-64, 73, 76, 117
Columbia Fur Co: 146-50, 152-55, 157-64; establishes posts in upper Missouri Valley, 160; opens St. Louis office, 160
Columbia River: 25-26, 59, 76, 87, 90, 92, 97-103, 138, 148, 175, 241
Columbia River Fishing & Trading Co: 234
Comanche Indians: 217
Constitution (U.S. frigate): 91
Council Bluffs: 17, 112-13, 127-28, 162, 187, 191, 194
Crooks, Ramsay: 17, 89, 95, 97, 100, 103, 118, 125, 141-42, 144-45, 147, 149-50, 152-54, 156-59, 161, 163-64, 220, 222, 231-32
Crow Indians: 58-61, 73, 98, 126, 161, 186, 197, 216, 225, 228, 230

Day, John: 100
Delauney, Pierre: 79, 99
Desire, Jacques: 117
DeSmet, Pierre-Jean: 115, 117, 127-29, 219

Detaye, Pierre: 99
Devil's Rake: 116
Dickson, Joseph: 13-16, 53, 57
Dorion, Pierre, Jr: 54, 96, 98, 100
Drips, Andrew: 145
Drouillard, George: 51-52, 61, 65, 75
DuBourg, Bishop: 108
Dubreil (Astorian): 79
Dunbar, William: 38

Fitzpatrick, Thomas: 189, 199, 202, 225, 230-31, 234, 236, 240-41
Fitzpatrick, Sublette and Bridger: 241-42
Flathead Indians: 61, 77
Fontenelle, Lucien: 240-42
Fort Atkinson: 191, 199
Fort Chartres: 16
Fort Hall: 241
Fort Henry: 186-88, 190-91, 197
Fort Jackson: 228
Fort Kiowa: 196-97, 199
Fort Laramie: 211, 219, 239-40, 242 (see also Fort William)
Fort Leavenworth: 112, 231
Fort Lisa: 57, 60-61, 64, 73-75, 77
Fort Lookout: 150
Fort McKenzie: 227
Fort Mandan: 73, 77
Fort Manuel: 61
Fort Miro: 38
Fort Osage: 72
Fort Pierre: 24, 124, 130, 226
Fort Raymond: 61
Fort Recovery: 150
Fort Snelling: 159
Fort Tecumseh: 123-24
Fort Union: 118, 120, 124, 126, 132, 226-27, 229, 231
Fort William: 227, 230, 241-42 (see also Fort Laramie)
Fraeb, Henry: 234
Freeman, Thomas: 39
Fulton, Robert: 109

Fur Trade: 20-21, 24, 29-30, 35, 38, 46, 55, 65, 79, 112, 122, 137, 151, 157, 168, 172-73, 175, 237-38; superiority of British goods, 67-68; weapons, 48; dress of fur trader, 48; St. Louis leaders, 34-36, 51, 55, 65-68, 86-88, 114, 138-41, 144, 153, 221

Gallatin River: 61
Gardner, Johnson: 202-04
Grant, Pres. Ulysses S: 219
Gratiot, Charles: 137-40, 142-43
Great Salt Lake: 79, 203
Green Bay: 146
Green River: 26, 59, 61, 66, 77, 176-77, 200-01, 204
Gros Ventres Indians: 126, 197, 229

Ham, Zachariah: 202
Hancock, Forrest: 13-16, 53, 57
Hempstead, Thomas: 145, 181
Henry, Andrew: 73, 75-77, 117, 167, 171-72, 174, 178-80, 182, 185-88, 190-91, 194-95, 197-98
Henry's Fork: 76, 201-02
Henry's Lake: 76
Hoback, John: 79, 97, 99
Hoback River: 77
Hudson's Bay Co: 146, 178, 202-06
Hunt, Wilson Price: 89, 95-97, 99, 100
Hunter, George: 38

Immel, Michael E: 150-51
Indians: prehistoric trade, 19 (see also tribe names)
Irving, Washington: 95

Jackson, David E: 164, 189, 202, 207
Jackson's Hole: 59-60
Jefferson, Pres. Thomas: 37-39, 50, 83-84, 86-87
Jefferson River: 61-62, 64
Jesseaume, Rene: 50

Jones, Ben: 97, 103
Jones, Robert: 145, 150-51

Kansas River: 112
Keelboats: 47, 108, 110-11
Kimball, Lt. Joseph: 54
Kipp, James: 146, 160

LaBarge, Joseph: 117, 132
LaChapelle (Astorian): 79
Laidlaw, William: 146
Lamazee (ship's interpreter): 93, 95
Lamont, Daniel: 146, 159
Landry (Astorian): 79
Laramee, Joseph (?): 239
Laramie River: 211, 214, 216, 237, 239
Larpenteur, Charles: 230
Leavenworth, Col. Henry: 191, 194-96
Leclerc, Francois: 103
Lee, Daniel: 236
Lee, Jason: 236, 239
Lewis (ship's clerk): 94-95
Lewis, Meriwether: 13-14, 25, 37, 42, 46, 50-51, 53-54, 57, 62, 65, 71-72, 78, 87, 90, 138
Lewis and Clark: journals, 13
Lewis Lake: 60
Lewis River: 60
Liguest, Pierre Laclede: 16
Liquor: 229
Lisa, Manuel: 17, 34, 50-57, 61, 65-66, 73, 117, 144-46
Little Sioux River: 16
Livingston, Robert R: 109
Logan, Ephriam: 201
Louisiana Gazette: 72
Louisiana, District of: 32
Louisiana Purchase: 109
Louisiana Territory: 31-32, 37-38, 55, 85-87

McDougall, Duncan: 89, 99, 101-02
McKay, Alexander: 89, 91, 93-94, 97

McKenzie, Donald: 89, 95, 97, 100-01, 174-79
McKenzie, Kenneth: 118-20, 125-26, 146, 149, 154, 157, 159-63, 227-33
McLellan, Robert: 16, 89, 98, 100, 103
McTavish, John George: 101-03
Madison River: 61
Mandan Indians: 23, 50, 53-56, 71, 73, 78, 96, 113, 130, 160, 162, 185-86, 226, 229-30
Marias River: 116
Maxent, Laclede & Co: 16, 33
Menard, Pierre: 51, 73, 75
Menard & Valle: 153, 161
Michilimackinac: 144
Miller, Joseph: 79, 89, 95, 97, 99, 100, 103
Mississippi River: 32, 67, 89, 109-10, 137-38, 144, 146, 148, 153, 155
Missouri Fur Co: 66-67, 70-72, 78, 139-40, 145-46, 148-51, 181, 190, 194-95
Missouri River: 13, 23, 25-28, 33, 36, 49-50, 52, 54, 56, 67, 71, 73, 77, 79, 86-87, 96-97, 104-05, 108, 110-11, 113-14, 116-18, 120-26, 129-30, 132-33, 137-44, 146, 149-51, 153, 155-56
Missouri Territory: 36
Mitchell, D. D: 227, 229
Moore, Daniel S. D: 183-85
Morris, Gouvernor: 85-86
Morrison, William: 51
Mountain Men: 14-15, 24-31, 42-46, 59-62, 71, 78, 80, 97-98, 116, 124, 148, 167, 183, 195, 215-16; culture and economics, 17-18; varying characteristics, 45
Munson & Barnard: 147
Musselshell River: 116, 187-88

Nadowa Creek: 96-97
Niobrara River: 122

Nootka Sound: 93
North West Co: 16, 101-02, 146, 174-75, 178
Nuttall, Thomas: 96, 236

O'Fallon, Benjamin: 193-96, 205
Ogden, Peter Skene: 203-06
Omaha Indians: 16-17
Omega (steamboat): 132-33
Oregon Trail: 79, 214
Osage Indians: 51
Ouachita River: 38

Pacific Fur Co: 86, 88-89, 91, 95, 99, 101, 175
Pattie, Sylvester: 79
Pawnee Indians: 16, 216
Perch, Capt: 56
Perkins, Joseph: 145
Picatt, Honore: 146, 229
Piegan Indians: 126
Pierre (So. Dakota): 24, 226
Pierre's Hole: 59, 217, 219
Pike, Zebulon Montgomery: 39-41
Pilcher, Joshua 145-46, 149, 151, 181, 194-96
Pinch, Lt. Jeremy: 56
Platte River: 26-28, 52, 72, 79, 112, 118, 125, 150, 199-200, 204, 211, 240
Poplar River: 228
Population in early West: 36, 38
Potawatomi Indians: 127
Potts, Daniel: 188
Potts, John: 62
Powder River: 197
Prairie du Chien: 155, 159
Pratte, Emelie: 152
Pratte, Chouteau and Co: 233, 242
Provost, Etienne: 202-03
Prudhomme, Gabriel: 202
Pryor, Ensign Nathaniel: 54-55

Racoon (British warship): 103
Rendezvous system: 174, 176, 178, 197-98, 200-02, 207, 237; description of, 176-77; Ashley-Henry

plan, 180, 196; Green River Rendezvous of 1833, 224
Renville, Joseph: 146
Reynolds, Gov. Thomas: 218
Rezner, Jacob: 79, 97, 99
Riviere aux Trembles: 228
Robinson, Edward: 79, 97, 99
Robinson, Dr. James Hamilton: 40
Rocky Mountain Fur Co: 188, 217, 225, 230, 234, 236, 240-41
Roosevelt, Nicholas J: 109
Rose, Edward: 61
Roseman, Lt: 56
Ross, Alexander: 175

St. Charles: 50
St. Croix: 159
St. Joseph's Mission: 127
St. Louis: 16, 32-33, 42, 46, 54, 68-71, 90, 95-97, 103, 107, 110-12, 118-25, 127, 132-33, 137-43, 145, 147, 149, 152, 156, 233; contrast in living conditions, 34-36
St. Michael: 79, 99
St. Peters (steamboat): 129-30
St. Peters River: 16, 144, 160
Sandy River: 77, 200
Santa Fe Trail: 213-14
Shoshone River: 60
Sioux Indians: 15-17, 23, 53-54, 73, 78, 98, 190, 194, 211, 216, 240
Sire, Capt. Joseph A: 117, 132, 133
Smith, Jedediah S: 79, 164, 183, 186-88, 190-91, 197-200, 202, 205, 207, 217, journal of, 184, 186 88
Smith, Jackson and Sublette: 217
Smith River: 188
Snake Indians: 77
Snake River: 26, 59, 77, 98-100, 175-77, 202, 241
South Pass: 77, 198-200, 204, 224-25
Spokane River: 101
Stinking Water River: 60
Stone, Bostwick & Co: 145-47, 152-55

Stuart, David: 89, 91
Stuart, Robert: 79, 89, 91, 101, 103-04, 141-42, 160, 220
Sublette, Milton: 225-27, 236, 240-41
Sublette, William L: 164, 189, 202, 205, 207, 217-18, 225-27, 231-32, 236-37, 239-41
Sublette and Campbell: 219-23, 225-28, 230-36, 241-42
Sweetwater Canyon: 198

Targhee Pass: 76
Teton Indians: 15
Teton Mountains: 59
Teton Pass: 60
Thompson, David: 56
Thorn, Capt. Jonathan: 91-94
Three Forks: 57, 61-62, 66, 73, 179, 199; stockade at, 74
Tilton, William P: 146, 160
Tilton & Co: 146
Tonquin (ship): 90-91, 93-95
Townsend, John: 236
Trade trails: 25, 29-30, 34, 212-16, 239
Turcot (Astorian): 79
Two-gwo-tee Pass: 59

Uinta Mountains: 176
Union Pass: 98

Vallar, Andri: 103
Verendrye, Francois: 23, 98
Verendrye, Louis Joseph: 23, 98
Verendrye, Sieur de la (Pierre Gaultier de Varennes): 23-24
Virgin, Thomas: 202

War of 1812: 78, 101-03, 138, 140-41, 144, 171-72
Weber, John H: 202
Weber River: 204
Westport: 130
White River: 150, 196
Wilkinson, Gen. James: 38-40, 66

Wind River: 58, 66, 98, 198, 228
Woods, Andrew: 145
Work, John: 204
Wyeth, Nathaniel: 203, 225, 231, 233-37, 239-41

Yankton Indians: 16, 54
Yellowstone Lake: 60
Yellowstone (steamboat): 121-27
Yellowstone National Park: 60

Yellowstone River: 13-14, 26-28, 53-54, 56-57, 68, 97, 116, 118-19, 125, 130, 179, 186, 205, 228
Young, Capt. B: 122
Young, Ewing: 79

Zebulon M. Pike (steamboat): 107, 110, 111-12, 114-15, 120, 133
Zenoni, John B: 145

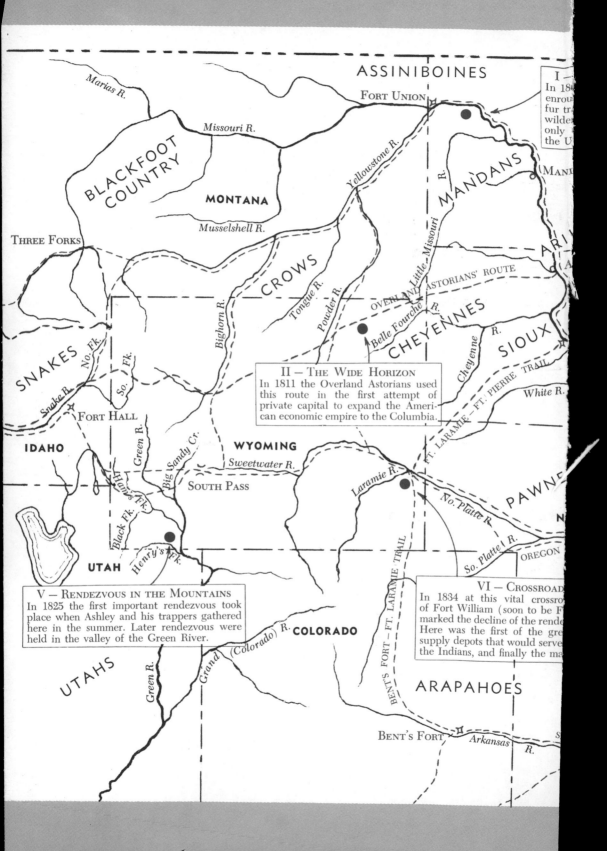

II — THE WIDE HORIZON
In 1811 the Overland Astorians used this route in the first attempt of private capital to expand the American economic empire to the Columbia.

V — RENDEZVOUS IN THE MOUNTAINS
In 1825 the first important rendezvous took place when Ashley and his trappers gathered here in the summer. Later rendezvous were held in the valley of the Green River.

VI — CROSSROAD
In 1834 at this vital crossro of Fort William (soon to be F marked the decline of the rende Here was the first of the gre supply depots that would serve the Indians, and finally the ma

I —
In 18
enrou
fur tr
wilder
only
the U